★ THE AMERICAN ADVENTURE SERIES ★

COWBOYS AND CATTLE TRAILS

By SHANNON GARST
and
WARREN GARST

EMMETT A. BETTS, *Editor*
Director, The Betts Reading Clinic
Haverford, Pennsylvania

Illustrations by
JACK MERRYWEATHER

WHEELER PUBLISHING COMPANY
CHICAGO

THE AMERICAN ADVENTURE SERIES

PORTUGEE PHILLIPS AND THE FIGHTING SIOUX

FRIDAY—THE ARAPAHO INDIAN

SQUANTO AND THE PILGRIMS

PILOT JACK KNIGHT

ALEC MAJORS

CHIEF BLACK HAWK

DAN MORGAN—RIFLEMAN

★ COWBOYS AND CATTLE TRAILS

KIT CARSON

BUFFALO BILL

WILD BILL HICKOK

DAVY CROCKETT

DANIEL BOONE

FUR TRAPPERS OF THE OLD WEST

THE RUSH FOR GOLD

JOHN PAUL JONES

△

Table of Contents

Texas Cowboys

1.	ON HIS OWN	1
2.	BAR XL RANCH	9
3.	THE COW HUNT	20
4.	WILD HORSE ROUNDUP	34
5.	A COWBOY PROMISE	42
6.	THE WINTER CAMP	52
7.	RIDING THE LINE	64
8.	MIDNIGHT ON THE RANGE	73
9.	A NORTHER STRIKES	81
10.	THE GOLDEN ONE	92
11.	DRIFTING	104

The Trail Drive

12.	TEXAS LONGHORNS	114
13.	THE CHISHOLM TRAIL	123
14.	RED RIVER CROSSING	135
15.	WHOA HAWS AND BARBED WIRE	150
16.	TROUBLES ON THE TRAIL	163
17.	LAND OF ROPES AND SADDLES	176

New Cow Country

18.	YANKEE WEATHER	186
19.	RIDING, ROPING COWBOYS	198
20.	COW SENSE	208
21.	THE TERRIBLE WINTER	218
22.	GIRL OF THE OW	230
23.	TRAIL END	243
	PRONUNCIATION OF WORDS	252

BRAVE AND LOYAL *were the booted, spurred cowboys of the old cattle trails. Their lives were packed with daring adventure and hard work.*

One of the best of these men was John Benjamin Kendrick. He knew the wide open range and the long, dusty miles of the cattle trails. He knew the dangers and the lonely life of a cowboy.

Like all pioneers, the cowboys did their share in settling this great country of ours. With a "Hi! Yi! Yipee!" they rode and roped their way into American History.

SHANNON GARST
WARREN GARST
EMMETT A. BETTS

On His Own

FIFTEEN-YEAR-OLD John Kendrick looked around the log cabin. It was a crude cabin with only one room and a dirt floor. For more than a year he had lived here with his uncle and aunt. It had been home. Now he was leaving.

John picked up a small bundle of clothes. These and the clothes he wore were all he owned in the world.

He turned to his uncle and aunt. He smiled at them.

"Well," he said, "I'm on my own."

"I wish you would stay, John," said his aunt.

"You don't have to leave," said his uncle.

"You both have been kind to me," said John. "I am thankful for what you have done for me. But now I'm old enough to make my own way in the world."

1

"What will you do, John?" asked his uncle.

"I'm heading for the Bar XL Ranch. Maybe I can get a job there."

"What if you don't get a job?"

"I'll walk on to another ranch."

His uncle smiled. "Still want to be a cowboy?"

"Yes!" The answer was quick and sure.

"That's what you have said ever since you were a little fellow." John's uncle shook his head. "I hope you will have more luck than I have had." He drew a deep breath and held out his hand. "Good-by, John. Good luck."

"We will miss you," said his aunt. "Remember, John, you can come back to us. You will always be welcome."

She turned away, but not quickly enough. John saw the tears in her eyes.

"Don't worry about me," he said to her. "I'll get along."

"Oh, I know you will," she replied. "You are a good boy. People can depend upon you. Here, take this package of food."

"Thank you," John replied with a smile.

He took the package, and looked around the cabin once more. Then he walked to the door and opened it. He stepped out into the golden Texas sunshine.

He pulled the wide brim of his hat down to shade his eyes. As he started toward the road the family dog ran after him.

"No, Toby," said John. "You can't go with me this time. I'm leaving for good. Go back, pal."

The dog sat down in the middle of the road. There was a hurt look in his eyes.

The door of the cabin opened. John's uncle called, "Take the dog, lad."

"You mean I can have him?"

"He's yours. He would pine away without you."

"Oh, thanks. Here, Toby! Here, pal!"

The dog raced toward John, and nearly knocked him over with joy. Then waving good-by to his uncle and aunt, John was on his way. Toby ran along beside him.

As John walked down the dusty road he tried to whistle. But he couldn't. There was a big lump in his throat.

"Toby," he asked, "do you know what a dogie is? Well, that's what the cowboys call a motherless calf. And that's what I am—a dogie."

John's pretty, young mother had died when he was a baby. He wished he could remember her. His father had been a preacher. He had died in 1861 when John was four years old. The boy could dimly remember him as a tall, kindly man.

John's thoughts ran through the eleven years after his father's death. He had been passed around from one set of uncles and aunts to another. They had all been good to him. But they were poor people. He knew how hard it was for them to take care of their own families. John thought he was now old enough to take care of himself. Yes, sir! He could make his own way in the world!

His uncles lived on cattle ranches in Texas. Almost everyone in the state owned herds of cattle. Almost everyone was poor.

The only parts of the animals that had a market value were the hides and fat, or tallow. If the ranchers could have sold the meat, too, then they would have made a lot of money. But there were no railroads to ship the cattle to markets in the north and east.

Later John had heard about the men who drove their cattle north to Abilene, Kansas. Abilene was on a railroad. It was a great shipping point. Hundreds of thousands of cattle were shipped from Abilene to the eastern markets.

John had talked to cowboys who had driven cattle up the long, long trail to Abilene. The stories they told him were very exciting. He planned to make such a drive himself some day—after he became a cowboy. Oh, he planned to do many things in the days that lay ahead.

About noon John stopped to eat his lunch. He sat in the shade of a small tree.

"Here, Toby," he said, tossing a piece of corn bread to the dog. "Eat it slowly. Enjoy every bite. If I don't get a job at the Bar XL, I don't know when we will eat again."

Boy and dog shared the food. After they had eaten, they were on their way again.

The road was dusty. The sun was hot. But John didn't mind. His faithful friend was with him.

"I'm going to be a real cowboy—a top hand, Toby," he said. "I'll work hard and save my money and buy cattle. And maybe I'll have my own ranch some day. You'll be with me, Toby."

The dog wagged his tail as though he understood every word. John reached down and patted Toby's head. "We'll share all our adventures."

On and on John walked. He was tired. It was getting harder and harder to lift one foot and put it before the other. He was hot, dusty, and hungry, too.

The sun was setting. John was almost too weary to notice the wonderful blaze of colors. He was thinking that he and Toby might have to spend the night in the open.

Coming to the top of a low hill, however, he saw a group of log buildings. They were shaded by cottonwood trees. It was the Bar XL Ranch.

The thought of food, rest, water, and best of all—a job, took away the tired feeling.

John walked faster. He came to the fence around the main buildings. He let down the bars of the pole gate, and walked across the yard. He knocked on the door of a building.

A Mexican woman came to the door.

John asked, "Where is the boss of this outfit?"

"Boss away now," the woman replied.

John knew that when the boss of a ranch was away another man would be in charge. The man was called a foreman.

And so John asked, "Where is the foreman?"

"I cook for cowboys," the woman answered. "I not know where men work. Ah," she added, "there is foreman now." She pointed to a man on horseback who had just ridden into the yard.

For a second John looked into the kitchen. He was hungry and he could smell the food cooking. It made his mouth water. Then he turned and hurried to the tall, lean man on horseback.

"Do you want to hire a cowboy?" he asked.

The foreman looked the small, thin boy over

without answering. He swung lightly from his saddle to the ground.

"Aren't you kind of young and skinny to be a cowboy?" he asked. His blue eyes twinkled. A smile pulled at the corners of his mouth.

"I can ride and rope," said John quickly. "I'll do my best to make you a top hand."

"I doubt if I have a place for you." The man took off his big hat and scratched his head. "But I couldn't turn a dogie like you out at night. It's twenty miles on to the next ranch. I reckon you're hungry."

"I am, but what about a job? That's what I really want."

The man threw back his head and laughed. "What's your name, Son?"

"John Benjamin Kendrick."

"All right, John. I'll find something for you to do around here. By the way, my name is Rusty. Now, come with me. I'll have the cook give you something to eat."

"Oh, thank you." A smile flashed across John's face. "Come on, Toby," he called, "we're hired!"

Bar XL Ranch

JOHN felt better after he had eaten a big supper of roast beef, corn cakes, and dried apple pie. He thanked the cook for the food she had given him and Toby. Then, with his dog at his heels, he headed for the bunk house.

Rusty had told John to meet him at the bunk house. It was the building where the cowboys lived and slept. Right now they were singing and talking.

"You will sleep out here, Toby," John said when they reached the door. He patted the dog's head and stepped inside.

He glanced around the big room. Rusty was singing with a group of cowboys gathered around the fireplace. Other cowboys were seated at a table. A few were lying in their bunks built along the walls of the room.

John noticed that most of the cowboys were tall and strong like Rusty. Some of the men had on shirts of plain dark colors. Others wore bright colored shirts. All of the men tucked the legs of their trousers, or jeans, into the tops of their high-heeled boots.

John stood quietly, hat in hand. At last a cowboy saw him and called, "Howdy, Kid." Everyone in the room turned and stared at John.

"Rusty," asked a man, "is this the dogie you were telling us about?"

Rusty nodded. "Boys, meet John Benjamin Kendrick. I just hired him to do odd jobs around the Bar XL."

"Yipee!" a young cowboy shouted. "That's the best news I've heard in weeks!"

The room rang with laughter. John laughed, too. But he wondered why the young cowboy was so excited.

"Yipee!" the young cowboy slapped John on the back. "No more peeling potatoes for me! No more soap making! No more making candles! Yipee!"

So that was it! The smile on John's face was gone. He didn't want to do odd jobs! He wanted to be a cowboy—a real cowboy.

He turned to Rusty. The foreman was watching him closely.

"Still want the job?" Rusty asked. There was no twinkle in his eyes and no smile on his lips.

"Yes, sir." John answered quickly.

Rusty held out his hand. "Good for you, Kid," he said. "You'll get along all right." He pointed to a bunk. "Take that one. It's right over mine. It's yours as long as you work at the Bar XL."

John tossed his bundle of clothes up on the bunk. He grinned at the cheering cowboys.

"Boys," Rusty called, "it's time to turn in."

A few minutes later the bunk house was quiet. John, lying in his bunk, winked at a star shining in through the window.

"I'll be a cowboy yet," he whispered to the star. "No one—nothing—can stop me." Smiling to himself he fell asleep.

In the morning John was up and dressed before the cowboys awakened. The second he closed the bunk house door, Toby came running to him. Together they hurried to the cook house.

An hour later the cowboys came in for breakfast. John had already eaten and was hard at work. He grinned in answer to their jokes and rough good humor.

But the cook shook a big frying pan at the men. "You let young one alone," she said. "He nice boy."

"You bet he is," Rusty patted John on the shoulder. "Come on, boys." He strode on and took his place at the head of a long table.

While the cowboys ate breakfast John listened to their talk. Some were to spend the day breaking wild horses. Others were riding out to work on the range.

The range was the land where the cattle grazed. There were many, many herds of cattle on the range. Some of the herds belonged to the Bar XL. The rest of the herds belonged to other ranches.

The Bar XL cowboys were going to gather, or round up, their cattle. Then the men were going to mark their cattle to show that they belonged to the Bar XL. This work was called "branding."

How John wanted to be like the men! Just to hear them talk made his heart beat faster. How long would it be before he would ride with them, work with them?

Days passed and grew into weeks. And still John was the cook's helper and the ranch chore boy. He sawed and chopped and carried wood. He peeled mountains of potatoes. He washed stacks and stacks of tin plates and cups. He made candles by dipping string into melted tallow.

Every day he carried ashes from the ranch house and other buildings to a pit. He poured water over the ashes. The water dripped through the ashes into a wooden bucket to make a strong lye. He used the lye to make soap.

John worked hard. The hours were long. In spite of everything he was happier than he had ever been.

From the beginning John loved the Bar XL. He liked all the cowboys, and they liked him. Rusty, of course, was his best friend.

Then there was "Packsaddle." No one in the outfit knew his real name. He was a big, sturdy fellow who could ride like the wind. He could sing all the cowboy songs.

One night in the bunk house John was singing with the cowboys. The door opened and a man entered the room.

"Howdy, boys," he called in a loud voice.

"Howdy, Boss," the cowboys shouted.

Rusty hurried to the boss, and the two men shook hands. They talked in low voices for a few minutes.

Then the boss called, "Boys, tomorrow some of you are to go on a cow hunt. Thirty-five hundred of my cattle are to be branded and driven to the Bar XL."

"What are you going to do with the cattle?" asked Packsaddle.

"I sold them to a man who is driving them up the trail to Abilene," the boss replied. "Well, that's all, boys. Rusty will give you your orders."

The boss left. For a while the room was quiet. Cowboys sat staring into space.

"Fellows," said Packsaddle, "it's a shame the boss doesn't drive his own herd up to Abilene. That's how you make money in the cattle business."

Rusty nodded. "The boss says he is too old to make the drive. It's a long, hard trip. Remember, the trail goes through the Indian country. Then, too, he might lose the entire herd in a stampede, or the cattle might drown crossing a river."

"I wish I had my own herd," said Packsaddle. "I'd make the trail drive."

"So would I," said Rusty. "Danger, hardships, Indians—nothing would stop me. I'd get the cattle to Abilene and sell them. Then I'd come back to Texas and buy another herd. Why, in three years I'd be rich!"

"Maybe," spoke up a cowboy. "But you might be dead."

"That's the chance I would have to take," said Rusty. "But if I had a herd—"

"Any man can get his own herd these days," broke in a cowboy. "All he needs is a long rope."

The men looked at one another. The cowboy, sitting next to the man who had spoken, rose to his feet and walked away.

John glanced at the men. He knew what they were thinking. They were thinking of the thousands of cattle that ran wild on the Texas range. The wild cattle were not branded. They were called "mavericks."

Some years before, Colonel Samuel A. Maverick had been given a herd of cattle by a man who owed him money. The colonel turned the herd over to a lazy fellow. He let the cattle run wild, and didn't even bother to brand the calves.

Some of Maverick's neighbors decided that if the colonel didn't want the calves, they did. They rounded up the calves, marked them with their own brands and kept them. Since then all cattle without a brand are called mavericks.

Many cowboys rounded up mavericks and started their own herds. To be sure it was stealing. But the cattle had little market value. Nothing was done to stop it.

Now times had changed. There was a market

for cattle in Abilene. Now cattle stealing was a crime.

A man who stole cattle was a cattle rustler. He was looked down upon by all honest cowboys. If he was caught stealing, he was likely to be hanged. And his own long rope, or lasso, was used to hang him.

Rusty stood up and hooked his hands in his belt. "Throwing the long rope isn't my line of business," he said. "I reckon I'll have to get rich the hard way. It will take longer, but I'll like myself better."

"You go your way. I'll go mine," the man growled. His eyes did not meet Rusty's steady gaze. "There are plenty of men who will go my way."

"No one in this outfit will go along with you," said Packsaddle.

"Oh, I wouldn't be so sure," the man replied. "What about it, boys?"

The cowboys shook their heads.

The man turned to John. "What about you, Kid?" he asked.

John held himself straight. "I want to be a cowboy. Some day I want to have my own herd. But I'll never throw the long rope, Mister. Never!"

The man snorted and walked away.

Rusty patted John on the shoulder. "Kid, I haven't been fair to you. I have made you work all this time as our chore boy. Those days are over, John. I'm going to start right now making a cowboy out of you. You are going on the cow hunt with us tomorrow."

John threw his hat into the air. "Yipee!" he shouted. "Yipee!"

———

1. Why did the Texas cowboys drive their herds of cattle to Abilene, Kansas?

2. What did John do at the Bar XL?

3. What did the cowboys do?

4. The following are some words the cowboys used. Tell what they mean.

outfit	dogie
ranch	maverick
top hand	range
roundup	brand
lasso	rustler

The Cow Hunt

RUSTY chose ten men to go on the cow hunt. He gave them his orders.

Then he turned to John. "The Bar XL has horses for its men," he said. "But each man must have his own outfit. Do you have a saddle and bridle?"

"No," John answered.

"Do you have a pair of chaps?" asked Rusty.

John shook his head. Chaps were the leggings the cowboys wore over their trousers. Cowboys had to wear chaps to protect their legs while riding in the brush country.

"Do you have a good, strong lasso?"

Again John shook his head. "I don't have an outfit," he said in a low voice.

"We'll take care of that," spoke up Packsaddle. "Boys," he called, "let's make up an outfit for this maverick of ours. What do you say?"

"Sure! Sure!"

"I'm a little runt like you, John," said a cowboy. "My boots will fit you."

"And you can have my old saddle and bridle,"
said another.

Leather chaps, long ropes, shirts, and jeans
were piled on the table. The men crowded
around John urging him to take his choice.

"If Rusty is going to make a cowboy out of you,
we want to help, too," they said.

John choked a little. "Thanks," he said. "You
know, I don't feel like a dogie or a maverick any
more."

"You're not, John," said Rusty. "You're one
of the boys of the Bar XL."

In the morning John and Rusty went to the
big pen, or corral, where the horses were kept.
Toby came bounding along with them.

"Toby would be a help on the cow hunt," said
John. "Maybe we ought to take him with us."

Rusty laughed. "All right, but keep him tied
when we brand the cattle."

At the corral the cowboys were throwing their ropes to catch their horses. The horses tried to dodge the whirling ropes. But one by one they were caught and saddled and bridled.

The horses were broken to ride and trained to work. After a night's rest, however, the cow ponies were full of snorts. Each morning most of them put up a stiff fight. They bucked and reared trying to unseat their riders. But it was all in fun. Soon the ponies settled down to the business of the day.

"Take the brown horse with the white star on his face," Rusty told John. "The one over there by the gate."

Slowly John walked toward the horse. He hoped the horse would not be hard to handle. The cowboys would laugh if he had any trouble.

"There! There!" John said quietly, keeping his eye on the horse. "You and I are going to be friends."

He was close enough to rub the horse's neck. But he did not try to touch the animal. He talked in a low, gentle voice. "Don't make any trouble this morning, old fellow," he said. "Any other time—but not this first morning."

The horse nosed John's shoulder. Quickly John slipped the bridle bit into the horse's mouth and pulled the bridle up over his ears.

He led the horse to the fence where the saddles were lined. He took the one the cowboy had given him and put it on the horse. He slipped his left foot into the stirrup and swung into the saddle.

"Come on," Rusty called to him. "You're riding up in front with me."

The cowboys rode south over the nearly level plain. Far away John sighted herds of cattle. They were thin, homely animals with slender legs and long, sharp horns. In fact, their horns were so long that the cowboys usually called them "Longhorns." They were wild as deer and they were fighters by nature.

Buffalo and wild horses, too, roamed the great stretches of grazing land. But to the cowboy this wide open, treeless country was cow country. This was range country, the land of ropes and saddles.

"John," said Rusty as they rode along, "a cow hunt is full of danger. But it's exciting work. Come to think of it, everything we do is exciting. I wouldn't trade places with the richest man in the world."

"Neither would I," John laughed with joy. "This is the life for me."

"Let me give you some advice, Son. I'm an old hand in this business. Almost anyone can learn to ride and rope. But to be a real cowboy—ah, that's different! A real cowboy never breaks his word. He is loyal to his outfit. He never forgets a friend."

"I will be a real cowboy," said John. "I give you my word."

The men rode all day, stopping only to rest their horses along the way. At sunset they came to a big corral. It was near a dense brush of mesquite.

Mesquite trees, except where they had plenty of water, did not grow very tall. Usually they were small shrubs with strong, crooked branches and great long roots.

The cowboys used mesquite for many things. They rested in its shade from the hot rays of the blazing sun. They used the wood for their campfires. They made posts and poles of mesquite for their corrals and fences.

The mesquite corral, near the brush, had been built by the cowboys of all the ranches in that section. They used the corral when they rounded up their herds on the range.

"We'll camp here," Rusty told his men. "We will hunt our cattle and drive them into the corral. Then we will brand them and drive them back to the Bar XL."

"Say, Rusty," called Packsaddle, "there are some longhorns in the brush. Let's drive them into the corral."

"All right, boys. Spread out!" ordered Rusty.

The cowboys raced their ponies into position. They formed a half circle around the mesquite. Then, shouting at the top of their voices, they dashed into the brush. The cattle were wild with fear. They came tearing out of the brush.

The cowboys were shouting. Branches were

breaking and popping like pistol shots. Cattle were bawling. Choking dust rose in clouds.

Before dark most of the cows had been driven into the corral. A few escaped, but the cowboys let them go.

"We'll get them later," they said.

While camp was made two men stayed at the corral. They rode round and round singing to quiet the cattle. Later their places would be taken by two other men. All night two cowboys would circle the herd.

In camp the men gathered around a campfire to cook supper. They were laughing and talking with one another.

Like the others, John was sitting on his heels. Toby was beside him, waiting for his share of bacon and corn bread.

John heard a cowboy ask Rusty, "What about the kid? Will he take his turn at guard duty?"

"No," was Rusty's low answer. "We'll make the cow hunt easy for him."

Quickly, John rose to his feet. He walked around the circle to Rusty and the cowboy.

"I don't want any favors, Rusty," he said. "I'll take my turn. I can do a man's work."

Rusty looked at the boy for a second without speaking. Then he said, "All right, John. Take your turn at midnight with Packsaddle. I hope you can sing better than he does."

"Say," laughed Packsaddle, "what's the matter with my singing? The cows love it!"

At midnight, John and Packsaddle left the sleeping camp. They mounted their ponies and rode to the corral. The two guards, who had been circling the herd, went back to camp.

"John," said Packsaddle, "the cattle are not used to being corraled. They may try to break out and run away."

"You mean they might stampede?"

"Yes, and that's why I want you to keep your eyes and ears open."

"I will, Packsaddle," said John.

"Good. Let's ride!"

Packsaddle rode off into the darkness. John touched his horse and started around the corral the other way. He listened to the sounds of the night. The cattle were moving slowly about in a close packed circle. Far away he caught the long, drawn-out howl of a coyote. All else was quiet.

John began to sing. He set the rhythm of the song to the slow, steady gait of his cow pony. Halfway around the corral he met Pack-saddle. As they passed each other they were both singing,

> "Come-a ti yi yipee
>
> Yipee yeh!
>
> Come-a ti yi yipee
>
> Yipee yeh! Yipee yeh!"

Two hours later their night watch ended. As they rode back to camp Packsaddle said, "You're all right, Kid. Keep on taking your turn. You'll be a top hand some day—or I'll miss my guess."

All during the cow hunt John worked with the men. Every morning he was up before dawn. Every night it was late before he fell asleep, tired but happy.

He rode with the men to hunt cattle on the

plains and in the brush country. He helped drive the herds into the corral.

He watched the cowboys drive the cows and their calves away from the rest of the herd. To "cut out," as the cowboys called the job, was hard work. But it had to be done. The calves had to be cut out, so they could be branded with the Bar XL brand.

Sometimes the cattle were branded on the plains. But it was easier to do the job in a corral. The cattle to be branded were driven into a narrow chute with two strong gates.

John's job was to open the first gate. As soon as a cow and calf were driven into the chute, he closed the gate. Then another cowboy opened the second gate and let the mother cow out into the corral again. The bawling calf was kept locked in the chute to be branded.

Rusty, Packsaddle, and two older cowboys did most of the branding. They worked quickly and with skill.

John watched them. He hoped they would let him help. But they paid little attention to him.

After two days of hard work, there were only a few calves left to be branded.

"Say, John," asked Rusty, "do you want to try your hand at this job?"

"Yes." John ran to the mesquite campfire near by. He took a long, red-hot branding iron from the glowing fire.

He raced back to the corral and climbed up on the fence. He leaned over and placed the iron on the calf's left hip.

The bawling calf bawled even louder as the iron burned into its hide. In a few seconds John lifted the iron. He had made a good clean brand.

"You ran the iron like a top hand," praised Rusty. "Everyone will know this calf belongs to the Bar XL."

"The brand won't mean a thing to Jed Dorn," spoke up Packsaddle.

"Jed Dorn?" questioned John. "Who is he?"

"Oh, Jed claims to be a buffalo hunter," answered Packsaddle. "He shoots buffalo and sells the hides. But everyone around here thinks he makes most of his money with a long rope."

"Jed is clever," said Rusty. "So far, the only cattle we have found him branding are mavericks."

The men talked on while they worked. At sunset they finished branding the calves. Dog tired, they cooked their supper. Then they rolled up in their blankets and were soon asleep.

In the morning the men started driving the cattle back to the ranch. Toby was a great help in the drive. He raced after the cows that were trying to run away. He nipped at their heels until the cowboys came dashing up to guide them back to the herd.

"Your dog is worth about three men when it comes to herding cattle," said Rusty. "I'd like to buy him from you, John."

"Oh, I couldn't sell Toby. He is my partner."

Rusty laughed. "I didn't think you would sell him. Say," he asked, "did I tell you that I'm taking the herd up the trail to Abilene?"

"No! That's wonderful, Rusty!" exclaimed John. "I don't know enough about herding cattle yet. But when I'm a real cowboy I'll make the trip, too. When will you leave?"

"After the wild horse roundup."

"Oh, I'm glad you will be here for the round-up."

"So am I. It's the most exciting event of the year."

"I'll miss you when you go, Rusty. I'll miss you like everything."

They rode along in silence. At last Rusty said, "There won't be much to do at the ranch after the cattle go up the trail. Most of the cowboys will drift south. I'll speak to the boss to keep you on—"

"I don't want any favors," broke in John. "I can take care of myself."

"You have already shown that you can stand on your own two feet, Kid," Rusty grinned. "But can't a fellow help his best friend?"

Wild Horse Roundup

THE Bar XL cowboys were looking forward to the wild horse roundup. At last the day came. At three o'clock in the morning, the cook banged on a dishpan with a big spoon. The men grumbled as they pulled on their jeans and boots. None, however, wanted to miss the roundup.

After a quick breakfast, the men saddled their horses and set out. John rode beside Rusty.

"Cowboys wouldn't be cowboys without horses," said John as they galloped over the plains.

"You're right," laughed Rusty. "A cowboy on foot is a sorry animal. Do you know how the first horses and cows came to the western plains?"

"Yes," John answered. "The Spaniards brought them to Mexico. Later the Spaniards crossed these very plains. Some of their cattle and horses were lost or stolen by the Indians."

"Yes, and those horses and cattle started the great herds that are here today."

"Horses made a big difference to the Indians in the plains country," John said.

"That's right. The Indians used dogs to haul their tepees and camp outfits. It was slow going. The Indians couldn't wander very far. When they learned to use horses, they became a power on the plains."

Rusty rose up in his stirrups. "There they are, boys," he said. "There is our herd of wild horses."

John looked across the plains. Far away there was a cloud of dust. As yet, it was all he could see.

"Come on," Rusty shouted to the men. "Drive them to our trap in the Red Rocks. Make a circle, boys."

Every man knew his job. Each one set spurs to his pony and went galloping toward the cloud of dust.

At first John thought that Rusty might be wrong. The cloud of dust could be raised by a herd of buffalo. But as it came closer, he saw the herd of wild horses.

John noticed that most of the wild horses were of different shades of brown. There were forty or fifty horses and colts in the herd. The leader was a big, strong, rust-colored horse with a black mane and tail.

Already some of the cowboys had ridden around the wild horses. Whooping, hollering, the cowboys soon had the herd galloping toward Red Rocks.

Slowly the circle of cowboys closed in, driving the wild horses closer and closer to the trap. The wild horses were wearing themselves out by useless plunges and zigzag dashes.

The herd was slowly driven toward a canyon formed by the red rocks. Here a clever trap, a gate of mesquite, had been built at the mouth of the canyon.

At last the tired horses were driven into the canyon. Rusty rode up and pulled the ropes that swung the gate shut. The wild herd was trapped in a large natural corral.

"Now the fun will begin," said Packsaddle. "Breaking a wild horse to ride! That's the sort of job I like best."

The Bar XL cowboys looked over the herd. Each man thought he knew all about wild horses, or "mustangs" as they were often called. Each man wanted to choose the best mustang in the herd.

"Rusty," said Packsaddle, "that rust-colored leader over there is about the color of your hair. It would be a good match."

Rusty nodded. "I've been watching him. He is the one I want. Open the gate, boys."

The gate swung open. Rusty rode in, his rope ready in one hand.

The mustangs were afraid. They crowded to the back of the canyon. But the rust-colored leader stood his ground. He neighed a warning and pawed the air with his forefeet.

Slowly, Rusty rode forward. Packsaddle and another cowboy entered the corral. They stayed near the gate. They held their ropes ready. The rest of the cowboys dismounted, and climbed up on the gate to watch. Two men loosened the six-shooters in their holsters.

It was plain that Rusty was in danger. But this was to be his own show, unless he needed help.

Now the leader screamed another warning. He advanced to meet this thing who might take away his freedom and the freedom of his herd. He reared up on his hind legs. He pawed the air with sharp front hoofs.

Rusty and his cow pony were ready. Rusty was out from under those sharp hoofs in a split second.

His right arm circled. His rope snaked out. The loop swung around the leader's forefeet. A quick jerk and the mustang fell to the ground.

Rusty's cow pony held the rope tight while Rusty leaped to the ground. He had a short rope in his hand. Before the mustang could get up, all four feet were tied together.

Packsaddle shook his head. "That's the way

we tie cows," he said. "But that's the first time I ever saw a man tie a wild horse."

"Why?" asked John.

"Most men aren't quick enough," Packsaddle replied. "A wild leader is just about as mean as any animal I know. He is quick with his hoofs and quick with his teeth. I don't care about mixing with the leader of a wild herd."

By this time Rusty had a lasso around the mustang's neck. He signaled to a cowboy to bring him a saddle. Quickly the two men slapped the saddle on the fighting mustang.

"Well, I'll be a dogie's uncle!" exclaimed Packsaddle. "Rusty is going to do the whole job at once! He's going to ride him!"

The cowboy slipped the rope off the leader's legs. The animal leaped to his feet. Rusty was already on his back.

For a moment the leader stood still. Then he exploded into action.

John had seen horses buck before, but never like this one. He feared Rusty's head would be snapped off by the quick jumps and twists.

It seemed to John that the struggle went on for hours. But the leader could not rid himself of the thing on his back. Now he was tiring.

At last the bucking ceased. The mustang lowered his once proud head. John could not help feeling sorry for the handsome animal who had bowed to the will of man. His days of freedom were gone—forever.

Now that Rusty had mastered the leader, the other cowboys began to rope their mustangs. Most of the men roped their horses around the neck. They tightened the lassos until the animals quit fighting from lack of breath. Then the lassos were loosened. But the ropes were tightened whenever the fighting started again.

At length the wild horses stopped fighting the cruel ropes. After this, the feel of a lasso quieted a mustang who had learned the lesson of the rope.

The job of breaking the wild horses went on for days. John tried hard to do a man's work. But, as yet, he was not able to master a wild horse.

Rusty said to him, "I'm glad to see you have a way with horses. If you didn't, I wouldn't give two cents for your chances of making a top hand."

At last the work was finished. Not all the mustangs were broken. The cowboys broke only the ones they thought would make good cow ponies. The rest were cut out and chased toward the hills.

Now the mustangs were bunched together and driven toward the ranch. It wasn't an easy job. Once outside the corral the mustangs smelled the air of freedom again. The wide open plains, the rolling hills called to them. Some made a break for liberty. But most of them stayed in line.

One reason why the mustangs held together was because Rusty was riding their leader. It was their habit to follow him.

At last, they were driven into the great pole corral of the Bar XL. Their days of freedom were over. Their life of service was about to begin.

A Cowboy Promise

THE wild horse roundup was over. Then the man who had bought the herd of cattle came to the Bar XL. He had ten of his own cowboys with him. They were riding good horses. They also had some extra horses with them. But even with the extra horses they did not have enough to make the trail drive to Abilene.

On long trips each cowboy used from six to eight horses every day. These horses he called his "string." He took good care of them, and seldom let anyone else ride them.

"I'd like to buy some of your mustangs," the man said to the boss of the Bar XL. "That is, I'll buy them if they are broken to ride."

"Well," the boss laughed, "they are still pretty wild. But my cowboys can ride them."

"Then so can mine," the man smiled.

"All right, boys," he called. "Go to the corral. Rope the horses you want for your strings."

John followed the cowboys to the big corral. The men began to draw numbers from a hat. They would rope in turn.

"Say, fellows," a cowboy shouted, "look at that rust-colored mustang. Man alive, isn't he a beauty!"

"That's Red," spoke up the boss of the Bar XL. "Rusty caught him in the wild horse roundup."

Red was certainly the prize horse in the corral. Already, under Rusty's careful training, he had become a good cow pony.

From all the talk, it was clear that every cowboy wanted Red in his string. John, of course, hoped that Rusty would draw number one from the hat. If he didn't, he would lose the horse he had trained and loved.

There was a worried look on Rusty's face as he took his number. John hurried to him.

"Did you get number one?" he asked.

Rusty shook his head. "Four," he answered. He looked over at his horse in the corral.

"Then someone else will rope your horse. What will you do, Rusty?"

"There isn't very much I can do," Rusty replied without taking his eyes off Red. "I'll just have to trust to luck."

While they were talking a tall, mean-looking cowboy joined them. "Your luck ran out, Rusty," he said. "I drew number one. I'm roping that horse for my string."

"You can't do it!" John exclaimed. "Red belongs to Rusty."

"Not any longer," the cowboy snapped.

Packsaddle came striding forward. "Just a minute! I don't know how your outfit does things. But on the Bar XL we believe in fair play. If a man has broken and trained a horse, the rest of us keep hands off that horse."

"I have number one," the cowboy sneered. "And I have taken a liking to Red. I'll rope him, and you can't stop me."

"No, we can't stop you," Rusty agreed. "But

I warn you. Be good to Red or you will settle with me."

"Men," the loud voice of the Bar XL boss made them turn, "what's this quarrel all about?"

Rusty reached into a vest pocket for his purse. "I'd like to buy Red," he said.

"Oh, so that's it," the boss smiled. "I can't say I blame you. All right, Rusty, I'll sell him to you for fifty dollars."

"I'll give you seventy-five," said the cowboy.

"No," the boss shook his head. "My offer to Rusty stands."

Rusty counted out the money and handed it to his boss. John noticed the purse Rusty put back into his pocket looked pretty thin and limp. But the wide grin on Rusty's face made everything all right again.

"Now get going," the boss ordered. "Rope your horses."

While the men picked out their mustangs, John sat on the top rail of the corral gate. It was fun to watch the cowboys and listen to their jokes and talk.

From his high seat, John had a good view. Far away, he sighted a covered wagon coming toward the ranch. The driver of the wagon had his team of horses at full gallop.

"That must be the cook for this outfit," John said to himself.

On long drives, cowboys did not cook their own meals. They had all they could do to take care of the cattle. Their boss hired a man to do the cooking. And all during the trip, the cook was the most important man in the outfit.

His wagon, or "chuck wagon" as it was called, was the center of cowboy life on the long trail. The chuck wagon was a kitchen on wheels. It was packed with food supplies, pots, pans, and tin dishes. Sometimes it even carried the blankets and extra clothing of the cowboys.

John waited until the chuck wagon rattled to a stop near the corral. Then, he jumped down from the gate, and headed across the stretch of ground to talk to the cook.

"Say, Kid," a cowboy called to him, "tell that old woman to get busy."

"I'll tell him exactly what you said," John replied.

"Oh, don't do that!" exclaimed the cowboy. "Never call the cook an old woman to his face. He is the best shot in the outfit and he doesn't go in for jokes."

John began to grin. "I know."

"Why, you rascal!" the cowboy laughed. "You almost scared the chaps off me."

John laughed, too, and strode on whistling. When he reached the chuck wagon, the cook was already at work.

"Howdy, young one," the cook said. "Are you going up the trail with us?"

"No," John answered with a sigh. "I wish I were making the trip."

The cowboy-cook moved about, talking and working. In a short time, he had the noonday meal ready. He placed a stack of tin plates and some tin knives, forks, and cups on his work table.

"Here," he said, handing John a plate. "Help yourself to the chow." Then in a loud voice he

called to the men of the outfit, "Come and get it!"

The hungry cowboys did not have to be called again. They rushed to the chuck wagon. They piled their plates high with thick slices of fried bacon, boiled potatoes, and big white onions. The pan of corn bread, which John thought would feed an army, was gone in a twinkling.

The men ate in a hurry. They drank cups of coffee, hot and black and strong as lye. Then they returned to the corral. The cook was surrounded by dirty dishes, pots, and pans.

John wanted to help wash the dishes. But the cook said, "No, I do my own work. I don't like to have anyone fussing around my chuck wagon."

He grinned and added, "That's the way an old woman acts, isn't it?"

"Maybe," John laughed. "But I have never seen a woman wearing a pair of six-shooters while she does her work."

"You're all right, Kid. Now, get going. I have work to do."

John joined the men riding out to the cattle corral. They had to brand the cattle with the new owner's mark before they started up the trail.

Rusty explained to John that this was the road brand. "We won't burn the brand into the animal's hide this time," he said. "It will only be burned into the hair."

"Why?" questioned John.

"Well, this is not a ranch brand. It is a road brand. It is only needed for the trail drive."

It took two days of hard, steady work to mark the cattle with the road brand. But at last the herd was ready. It was time for John to tell Rusty and Packsaddle good-by.

"I'll be waiting to hear all about the drive," he said to them.

The cowboys looked at each other. Then Rusty cleared his throat. "We may not come back to the Bar XL," he said. "If we like it up north we are going to get jobs on a ranch in Wyoming."

"Oh," was all John could say.

"So long," Packsaddle held out his hand. "Don't forget, I'm expecting you to be a real cowboy."

"I won't forget," John replied, shaking hands with his friend.

As Packsaddle hurried away, John said, "I don't want to stay here. Can't I go with you?"

"I am surprised, John. I thought you could take whatever came your way. That's what a real cowboy does. He takes it smiling—good luck and bad."

"I guess I had that coming," said John. He forced himself to smile, and then looked up at Rusty. "We will meet again some day, won't we?"

Rusty placed an arm around John's shoulder. "Yes, some day we will meet again. And when we do, we'll ride the range together. You can count on that, Cowboy."

———

1. Why did the cowboys sing to their cattle?
2. Tell about the wild horse roundup.
3. Who was the "old woman" of the outfit?

The Winter Camp

THE weeks raced by at the Bar XL. John was busy from morning to night. He rode and roped until he ached from the long hours in the saddle. In spite of the hard work, however, he was gaining weight and growing taller. He was healthy as a wild colt and as brown as an Indian.

ONE night after supper, John was told that the boss wanted to see him. He hurried to the ranch house. Toby, eager for their nightly frolic, trotted along beside him. But tonight John didn't feel like playing.

"Toby," he said, "the boss told some of the boys that he won't need them this winter. I hope that isn't what he is going to tell us."

When they reached the ranch house, John said, "Wait here." Then with quick, light steps he crossed the porch and knocked on the door.

"Come in," the boss called. "Come in."

Hat in hand, John entered. The boss was seated at a table in a corner of the room. He glanced up from a letter he was reading. Without speaking, he pointed to a chair. Then he went on reading the letter.

John sat down. He looked around the room. There wasn't much to see. There were a few chairs, a picture over the fireplace, and some books stacked on another table.

"Well, John," the boss said at last, "I suppose you are wondering why I sent for you."

"I think I know, sir. You won't need me this winter."

The boss shook his head. "No, I told Rusty I'd keep my eyes on you for awhile. You can stay, that is, if you want to be a line rider. You know what that means, don't you?"

"Oh, yes!" John exclaimed. "A line rider keeps the cattle of his herd within certain limits on the range."

"It's hard work," said the boss. "The cattle stray beyond the line. Then they have to be driven back to our range. Do you want to be a line rider this winter?"

"Oh, yes, Boss."

"Good."

The boss opened a box on the table. He took a pair of six-shooters and a holster from the box. "They are from Rusty," he said giving the guns and belt to John.

"From Rusty!"

"Yes, Rusty asked me to keep them for you until you would need them. And, John, you will need them this winter all right. I can't let you ride the line unless you are armed. There are too many buffalo hunters and cattle rustlers on the range. By the way, are you a good shot?"

"I'm a pretty good shot," John answered. He fastened the belt around his slim waist. "I never hoped to own a pair of six-shooters as fine as these. I wish Rusty were here so I could thank him."

The boss shook his head. "Rusty isn't coming back. He and Packsaddle are staying up north. It's tough luck to lose them. They are top hands.

Rusty was the best foreman I ever had. I'll miss him."

John swallowed hard. "I'll miss him, too. But I know we will meet again some day. Rusty told me we would."

"Then you will," said the boss. "Rusty has a way of keeping his word. Now, let's talk about your winter job."

"Yes, sir."

"I'm bringing some more cattle up from the south. With the herd will be a Mexican boy about your age. His name is Lopez. He doesn't speak much English, but he is a good cow hand. The two of you should make a good pair of line riders."

John grinned. "It will be fun living in a winter camp out on the range."

"Yes, when you are young it's fun," the boss said. "You are busy during the days. But the nights are long and lonely. That's why some cowboys won't ride the line during the winter."

John glanced at the books on the table. "I like to read," he said. Then he asked shyly,

"Could I take one of your books with me?"

"Why, of course. What kind of books do you like to read?"

"Oh, stories of adventure and of other countries and stories about Indians."

"I like them, too. I'll have a box of books ready for you."

"Thanks, Boss."

"Well, I guess that's all," the boss rose to his feet. "Be on the lookout for the herd. After it gets here, you and Lopez will head for the winter camp."

"I'll be ready," John promised.

A week later the herd came up from the south. John met Lopez, and at once liked the friendly, smiling Mexican lad.

While they were talking the boss joined them. "I'm glad to see that you two are friends already."

Lopez flashed a grin. "Toby my friend, too." His voice was soft and musical.

"We're leaving in the morning for the winter camp," said the boss. "I'm riding out with you.

The boys tell me that some buffalo hunters are out on the range near our camp."

"Rusty told me about Jed Dorn," said John. "He must be the meanest man in all Texas."

"Dorn is tough," the boss agreed. "Watch out for him."

Lopez patted the six-shooter in his wide, red sash. "We watch good," he said. "No buffalo hunter steal cows."

The boss laughed a little. He was serious, however, as he said, "I'm counting on you boys. But I don't want you to take any foolish chances. Good night. Be ready to leave at daylight."

Early in the morning, the little party headed south. John and Lopez raced their horses over the trail.

The boss, driving a supply wagon, came rattling over the trail. Toby was riding on the wagon seat beside the boss. Four sturdy cow ponies, tied to the wagon, trotted along behind.

Late that night the party reached the winter camp. The camp was in a grove of cottonwood trees. There were two log buildings: a cabin

for the boys and a shed for the horses. That
was all. It was the only camp for miles around.
There was nothing else except the open range.

"Well, boys," said the boss, "this is it. I hope
you like it, because you will be here a long time."

"It's fine," John replied quickly.

"Fine for cows and buffalo hunters," said the
Mexican boy. "Lopez like to sing and dance."

The three laughed, and set to work carrying the
supplies into the cabin. A candle was lighted.
Bed rolls and blankets were tossed up on the
two bunks. Bags of food and the box of books
were placed on a crude table. Cooking pots and
pans were stacked on the dirt floor near the fireplace. Other boxes of supplies were set in a
corner.

Then, while Lopez took care of the horses, John
cooked supper. The meal was eaten almost in
silence, for they were tired. Even Toby was
quiet.

"I'm going to hit the hay," the boss yawned.
"I'll take the lower bunk. You boys fight it out
for the other."

"We no fight," said Lopez. "John take bunk. Lopez sleep on floor."

John shook his head. "No," he said, "we're sharing everything and we're sharing alike. We will draw straws for the bunk."

"All right," the boss pulled a straw from the pad on his bunk. He broke the straw into a long and a short piece.

"The long straw wins," he said.

Lopez drew first, and drew the short straw. Grinning, he wrapped his blanket around him, and dropped down in front of the fireplace.

"I sleep good," he said. He looked up at John and winked. "Beds for ladies, not cowboys."

John threw back his head and laughed. "You can't insult me tonight. I'm too sleepy. Good night, Cowboy."

In the morning before the boss left, he gave his orders to the boys. "Keep the cattle on our range," he told them. "Every day one of you will ride west ten miles. The other will ride ten miles to the east."

"We will ride the line," said John.

"Storms and cold winds from the north will cause the most trouble," the boss went on. "Then the cattle will drift to the south. You must drive them back to our range.

"Buffalo herds will make trouble, too. They may make the cattle stampede. If this happens you may never find the cattle again."

The boss swung himself up on the wagon seat, and picked up the reins of his team. "I'll be out in a month with more supplies," he said. "From now on it's up to you. Keep the cattle on our range. Keep the buffalo off our range. That's all there is to it, boys. Good luck."

The boys watched the boss drive away. Then they went to the shed, and saddled their horses.

"Which way do you want to ride?" John asked.

Lopez shrugged his shoulders. "I no care. I go west today. Tomorrow, I go east."

"Fine." John mounted his horse and headed east. "See you tonight, Lopez," he called.

"For certain, my friend," the Mexican boy called in answer. "For certain."

John let his horse set his own pace. Like all cowboys, John loved his horse. A good cow pony is smart. A good cowboy trusts his horse. They work together as a team.

As John rode along, he studied the open range. For miles around he could see cattle grazing. Far to the south, a herd of buffalo was following its leader to a water hole.

At the end of the ten-mile line John came to a big mound of dead buffalo. Their great bodies had been skinned and left to decay and rot away.

"Jed Dorn must be around here somewhere," John said to himself. "But I won't worry about him as long as he stays off our range."

John started back to the camp. When he was near the cabin, he saw smoke curling up from the chimney.

"Lopez is cooking supper," he thought. "Good old Lopez."

Then he saw a horse—a strange horse tied near the shed. Quickly John reined in his cow pony, and slipped from the saddle.

He ran to the cabin and threw open the door.

There before the fireplace sat the dirtiest man John had ever seen. His buckskin clothes were greasy and stiff with blood. His hair and beard were matted.

The man rose to his feet. "Hello," he said. "Shake hands with Jed Dorn."

John made no sign that he saw the dirty, extended hand. He turned to Lopez.

"Why did you let him in?" he asked.

"Let him in!" Lopez exclaimed. "He here when I come back!"

"Surely you boys don't mind a visitor," spoke up Dorn. "It gets mighty lonely out here on the range."

"What do you want?" John demanded.

"Why, nothing!" Jed looked hurt. "I just want to spend the night with you."

"All right," John said. "You can stay tonight. But you are leaving in the morning—early."

Riding the Line

Jed Dorn rode away early in the morning.

Lopez took a deep breath. "I hope we see him no more. He bad man. He kill more than buffalo. I count six notches on his gun."

"I warned him to stay off our range," said John.

"He no afraid of two kids. He say so. He laugh at us."

"Jed didn't laugh when I told him we were dead shots. Say, are you afraid of that greasy buffalo hunter?"

Lopez did not answer at once. Then he shrugged his shoulders and smiled. "I no trust him."

"I don't either. But he is gone now and he may not bother us again. Come on, Lopez, let's ride."

The days at the line camp passed quickly.

There was always plenty to do. Riding ten miles out and ten miles back took up most of each day.

There were few days, however, when the boys rode only twenty miles. Often the cattle strayed and the line riders had to drive them back to their range. Other times, they had to ride hard to drive off herds of buffalo.

To drive off a buffalo herd was not an easy job. But usually loud shouting and a few shots from their six-shooters sent the herd stampeding.

Then, too, the boys spent some time hunting for food. Often, while driving a buffalo herd off their range, they would shoot a fat calf. They would take the best cuts of meat back to camp. Wild turkeys were plentiful. Now and then they shot a wild pig.

The boys took turns cooking the evening meals. Sometimes, after they had eaten, John would read a book aloud. On other evenings, Lopez would play his guitar and sing. The Mexican boy had a fine, clear voice. He loved to sing the folk songs of his home country.

"It is same as visit home," he said to John

one night. "Home, where I dance with pretty girls. Home, where I see no cows in sleep."

John laughed. "I'd rather dream about cows than about Jed Dorn. I dreamed about him last night."

Lopez threw up his hands. "Oh, that bad man! Why you talk about him?"

"I wish I could forget him. But I can't. I'm pretty sure that we will see Jed Dorn again."

"You think he come back for visit?" questioned Lopez.

"No," John shook his head. "That greasy buffalo hunter won't come back to visit us."

"Why you say we see him again?"

"I think he will try to rustle some of our cattle."

"You right," Lopez agreed. "Boss tell us to watch for bad man."

"Rusty and Packsaddle told me about Jed, too," said John.

"I hope we no see him."

"So do I," said John. "But we must be on the watch for him, Lopez."

"I do like you say, my friend. I watch."

The boys rode the line every day. The ride to the west was John's favorite. About five miles from camp was a bluff covered with mesquite. Wild cattle had beaten a trail to the top.

Every other day, John followed the trail to the top of the bluff. There he had a fine view of the country. He could see whether or not the Bar XL cattle had strayed or whether any buffalo herds were near.

One day, when John was on the bluff, he saw something far away. He stood up in his stirrups and shaded his eyes with one hand.

"It looks like the shadow of a cloud," he said to himself. "No!" he exclaimed aloud. "It's a herd of wild horses!"

He watched the wild horses come racing toward the bluff. When they were near, they stopped and began to graze.

John spotted the leader at once. He was a handsome horse. His golden coat shone in the sunlight. His mane and long, flowing tail were of a light cream color.

"Oh, you beauty," John said softly. "You beautiful, wild mustang."

The golden leader whinnied as though he had heard John's praise. The other horses stopped grazing. They pricked up their ears and snorted. The golden leader whinnied again. The whole herd broke into a gallop and raced away.

John sighed and touched his horse lightly with a spurred boot. "Come on, fellow," he said. "You're not much for beauty, but you'll take me where I'm going."

The sturdy little cow pony picked his way carefully down the rough trail. Once on the level ground he laid back his ears and raced over the line.

As John rode along he kept thinking of the golden leader. Maybe he and Lopez could trap the mustang. But he knew better. Two boys didn't have a chance to trap this proud beauty. Wild horses were wise animals.

Riding back to camp, John sighted some cattle south of the Bar XL range line. He spurred his pony toward them to see their brands.

The cattle were his, and so he swung his rope and shouted, "Hi! Yi! Yi!" Bellowing as though they were abused, the cattle headed to their own range.

On the way, John noticed a stretch of ground where the grass was matted down. The earth was cut with sharp hoof marks. He reined in his pony and slipped from the saddle.

While looking over the ground he came upon the ashes of a campfire. The ashes were cold. But the ground beneath was still warm. The fire had been built not long ago, perhaps early that morning.

John brushed the ashes from his hands. "Someone used this fire to work over brands," he said to himself. "And that someone is Jed Dorn."

John mounted his horse and followed the trail cut by the hoofs of the cattle. The tracks were hard to follow after the cattle had spread out on the range.

He rode on, hoping to find the stolen herd. But the only cattle in sight were quietly grazing. The sun had set sometime ago. It was growing dark. John turned his tired horse toward home.

When John entered the cabin, Lopez said, "You late, my friend. Why you gone so long?"

"Someone is rustling our cattle," John answered, hanging his hat up on a wooden peg.

"You joke—I hope."

"No," John replied. He went on to tell about finding the campfire and trailing the stolen herd.

As he finished he said, "I am sure this is the work of Jed Dorn."

"He has big nerve!" Lopez exclaimed. "He no wait to drive cattle away. He brand them under your nose. In morning, I ride to ranch. Tell boss."

"No, let's handle this ourselves."

"I do like you say. But we can do nothing this night. So eat good supper."

John shook his head. "I'm not hungry."

"Wait you see! Fat turkey all ready. After we eat, I show you new trick Toby know. He fine dog! Smart dog!"

John forced himself to smile. He knew the Mexican boy was only trying to be cheerful.

"All right, Lopez. Bring on your turkey."

While the two boys ate supper, they talked about the stolen herd. It was plain to see that Lopez wasn't too eager to catch a cattle rustler. He was willing to let well enough alone.

"Maybe you think this up," Lopez said hopefully. "Maybe flat grass made by buffalo."

"I suppose the buffalo built that campfire, too."

Lopez grinned. "Maybe."

"Now you listen to me," said John sternly. "It's our job to see that nothing happens to the Bar XL cattle on our range. This is the first important job the boss has given us. We are not going to let him down. If our job calls for danger, then we must face it together. Isn't that what friends do?"

The Mexican boy nodded. "You right. Tell Lopez what to do. He do like you say."

"Good! Now this is what we will do. Tomorrow we won't ride the line. Instead we will ride in a big circle around our range. We may be gone several days. We'll take our bed rolls and some grub with us."

"Maybe we find herd real quick."

"I hope so. But what I really want to do is to catch Jed Dorn."

"I wish I brave like you," Lopez sighed. "I feel 'shamed."

"You don't need to be ashamed. I'm scared, too. Plenty scared!"

"You joke," said the Mexican boy. "I no believe you scared. You say so to make Lopez feel good. Is that not so?"

"No, I'm telling you the truth, Lopez. I am scared."

"Then how you act so brave?"

John walked to the fireplace and placed another log on the fire. He stood quietly for a minute, staring at the dancing flames. Then he turned and faced Lopez.

"We can't let Jed Dorn call us a couple of kids and get away with it," he said. "No sir, that greasy buffalo hunter isn't going to scare us out of our jobs. We are going to keep right on riding the line for the Bar XL."

Midnight on the Range

Two days of hard riding brought no luck to the boys. They had found no traces of the stolen cattle or of Jed Dorn. Tired and hungry, they made camp near a small stream at the foot of a low hill.

They did not build a fire to cook supper. If the rustler was near, he might see the smoke. The boys were taking no chances. They ate another cold meal of corn bread and meat, sharing their food with Toby.

"Maybe tomorrow we have luck," said Lopez. "If no, maybe better tell boss. Buffalo hunter get far away."

John nodded. "I have been thinking about that, too. If Jed is hiding out somewhere then we are all right. But, if he is driving the herd up the trail, he already has a good start."

John tossed a piece of meat to Toby, and went on talking. "I would like to handle this by ourselves. But I don't want to lose the cattle. After all, they belong to our boss. I guess we will have to tell him."

"What you think he do?" questioned Lopez.

"He will hit the trail with all his cowboys. I am sure they will find the cattle and catch Jed Dorn, too."

"That I like to see!" Lopez grinned. "Where you go?" he asked as John started walking from camp.

"I want to look around while it is still light," John answered. "Come on, Toby."

At the mention of his name, Toby opened his eyes and quickly closed them again. Two days on the trail had given him all the chasing and running he wanted for a long time. For once he did not dash after his young master.

"Toby tired, like me," said Lopez.

John laughed and walked on alone. He followed the stream as it wound its way around the foot of the hill.

Not far from camp, the bank was covered with the hoof marks of cattle. More than likely the cattle had come to the stream for water, and then had gone on to graze. The earth was damp, showing that the cattle had been here not too long ago.

Carefully John looked over the signs. "Say, what's this!" he exclaimed.

Cut into the bank was the mark of a horse shoe. So the cattle had not come to the creek by themselves! They were being driven by someone!

John's heart pounded. He dropped to his knees and crawled along as he studied the ground. He was sure that at last he was on the trail of the stolen cattle. Better yet, he could find the hoof marks of only one horse.

"It's Jed's trail all right," he said jumping to his feet. "I must try to find where he has camped tonight."

John half walked, half ran up the hill. At the top, he looked all around.

About a mile to the north was a mesquite grove. John knew the place. During the cow hunt, he had helped drive a herd of wild cattle from the brush.

Evidently the Bar XL cowboys weren't the only ones who knew the place. A thin curl of smoke rose from the center of the grove. The smoke was a dead give away that someone was camped there.

John felt his blood run cold. "It's Jed!" He whispered the words. "I know it's Jed."

John hurried back to Lopez. "We're in luck," he said. "I have found Jed's camp."

Lopez threw up his hands. "You say that luck!"

"You bet I do," John grinned. "Don't you?"

Lopez shook his head.

"You aren't going to let me down, are you?"

"Who say I let you down?" questioned Lopez. "I just say it no luck to find bad man." He shrugged his shoulders. "Now, what we do, my friend?"

"We'll stay right here until about midnight," John answered. "Then we will ride to the grove. We will sneak in and catch Jed while he is asleep."

"Sound like good plan," said Lopez. "But maybe bad man wake up. He shoot us."

"We will have to take some chances, Lopez."

The boys waited quietly as the darkness of night settled over the range country. Stars began to twinkle. The moon came up bright and clear. Slowly the long hours dragged on.

Shortly before midnight John said, "Come on, Lopez. Let's go."

He patted Toby's head. "You can't go this time, old fellow. Wait here for us."

Without a word, the boys mounted their horses and headed for the grove. They rode slowly. They did not want to make too much noise. Near the grove they reined in their horses and slipped to the ground.

"We'll need plenty of rope," John whispered. "Take your lasso. I'll take mine, too."

Quiet as shadows, the boys moved into the grove. They inched their way along. They dared not move faster. A broken branch would pop like a pistol shot.

All around in the moonlight, they could see the dark forms of sleeping cattle. Ahead, there was a place where the ground was cleared of the brush.

And in the cleared spot, John saw the figure of a man asleep on the ground.

John nudged Lopez and pointed. "Jed!"

"For certain," Lopez whispered in reply. "I know loud snore he make."

"You grab his left hand," John whispered. "I'll grab his right one. Then, before he knows what has happened, we'll tie his hands back of him."

Lopez nodded. "I have rope ready."

They edged forward. Just as they reached the clearing, Jed rolled over and groaned. The boys froze in their tracks.

They didn't move until Jed was snoring again. Then, once more, they edged forward. Quiet as cats, they slipped up on Jed.

When they were standing over him, each grabbed a hand. Jed struggled to his feet. But before he could gather his wits, his hands were tied behind his back. He let out a roar that sent the cattle crashing through the brush.

"Say, what do you kids think you are doing?" Jed demanded.

"We're asking the questions, not you," John

replied. He jerked the six-shooter from Jed's belt. "Here, Lopez, keep him covered while I look around."

"This I like." Lopez took the gun.

"I'll get you two sneaking kids for this," Jed snarled. "I'll get even with you."

"Stand still," Lopez warned.

Now Jed changed his tune. "Why do you do this to me? I have done nothing to you boys."

"Nothing but run off with our cattle," John called. "Look!" He poked at a dead campfire with the toe of his boot. "Your branding irons are still in the ashes. You have been working over our brands."

"Everybody does that," Jed declared. "And if you were smart, you would, too."

John hurried back to face the rustler. "Some men brand mavericks," he said. "Maybe that's all right. But you were not branding mavericks, Jed Dorn, and you know it."

"Maybe I was careless," Jed admitted. "But I'll make a deal with you. Let me go and I'll pay you plenty."

"Nothing doing. We're taking you back to our cabin. And when the boss comes out with supplies, we're turning you over to him."

"You'll be sorry. I'll get even with you sneaking kids, if it's the last thing I do."

"Your threats don't scare me," John replied. "And another thing, Jed Dorn, you ought to be glad we are kids. We are going to give you a break. We are not going to hang you with your own long rope. We are going to let the law take care of you."

Jed snorted.

Lopez stepped closer to Jed. "You still say we kids?" he questioned.

John slapped the Mexican boy on the shoulder. "I'll get Jed's horse and his branding irons," he said. "Then we'll head for our camp. I wouldn't spend the night in this rustler's camp for all the cows in Texas."

"Or in Mexico," Lopez laughed softly.

A Norther Strikes

THE boys took their prisoner back to camp. At first, Jed ordered them to let him go. Then he begged to be set free. Neither John nor Lopez answered him. But Toby growled every time Jed raised his voice.

"We will have to watch Jed like hawks," John said to Lopez. "One of us must stay with him all the time."

"For certain," Lopez said.

"We'll take turns at guard duty. I'll take the first stretch."

"Good!" Lopez yawned. He glanced at Jed, lying on the ground a few feet away. "I no sleep near cow stealer. I sleep over there."

"All right," John chuckled. "I'll call you in two hours."

When Lopez was asleep the rustler said,

"You're a pretty smart kid, John. Did you get that Mexican out of the way so we can talk over our deal?"

For a second, John was so angry that he could not speak. Then he said, "I'll make no deal with you, Jed Dorn. And," he added, "that Mexican is my friend. We ride the line together."

Jed snorted, rolled over, and went to sleep. When he awakened, it was almost daylight. Lopez was on guard duty.

"He wake up," Lopez called to John.

"Good," John laughed. "Now you can have someone to talk to while Toby and I round up the herd. I want to be sure that the cattle are on our range before we start back to our cabin."

"I round up cows," said Lopez.

"We drew lots. Remember? I won!" John grinned, mounting his horse. He called to his dog and raced from camp.

John found the herd grazing near the mesquite grove. Slowly he circled the cattle. He rode close enough to see their brands.

Jed had done a clever job in working over the

Bar XL brands. But it was easy to spot the ones he had changed. The deep burns of the worked-over brands were still fresh. When the burns healed it would be hard to tell the brands had ever been changed.

"The cattle are all right," John said to himself. "They will stay on our range."

Just then from camp came the bark of a pistol. John gave his horse the spurs.

"What's the matter?" he shouted riding into camp at full gallop.

"He try to escape." Lopez waved his gun toward Jed. "I shoot in sky one time. He change mind."

"Jed," said John quietly, "we're taking you to our line cabin. It's a long ride. I hope you make it."

The rustler sneered. "What do you mean?"

"Just this—Lopez and I are dead shots."

The blunt warning must have given Jed plenty to think about during the ride to the cabin. He did not try to escape. But then he really didn't have a chance. All the way the boys kept their six-shooters ready.

The day was a perfect one for a long ride. It was sunny, and warm enough not to wear coats. Then, sometime late in the afternoon, a sudden gust of cold wind swept down from the north.

John and Lopez looked at each other. In one voice they exclaimed, "A norther!"

The gust of wind was the first sign of the coming storm. The wind blew harder. It began to turn cold. Clouds of sand whipped through the air. The sand cut John's face like so many sharp knives.

"Oh! Oh!" Lopez wailed. "Poor cows need us now."

"Let's get out of this!" Jed roared. "Let's make camp over there by that hill."

The boys stared at the rustler. Whoever heard of a cowboy thinking of himself when his herd might be in danger?

"We're not making camp," said John. "We're riding back to our cabin, even if it takes us all night."

The little party pressed on, stopping only to rest the horses. Toby was left behind.

"Poor Toby," said Lopez. "He get lost."

"Don't worry about that dog," laughed John. "He no keep up with us. Maybe storm so bad he no find line cabin."

"Toby will find our cabin all right," said John. "Toby is a cow dog."

Long after midnight, the boys and their prisoner reached the cabin. Never, the boys said, had the bare little shack been a more welcome sight.

But they could not enjoy the warmth of their blazing fire. They kept thinking about the cattle on the range. Where had they drifted? Would the cold wind bring snow and sleet?

Jed laughed at the boys. "The longer the norther lasts the better it suits me," he said.

"Buffalo hunter!" Lopez almost exploded in anger. "Cow stealer!"

John laughed. "Don't pay any attention to what he says."

"He make me mad!" Lopez replied. "He no care about cows in bad storm. Oh, poor cows!"

"As soon as it is light, I'm riding out to find our herd," said John. "I will—"

"I go, too," broke in Lopez. "We tie Jed up real good. We use more rope. He no get away."

John shook his head. "You will have to stay here. We can't leave Jed alone."

Lopez sighed. "I do like you say."

Shortly before John left, Toby was scratching on the door of the cabin. "Good old fellow," John hurried to the door. He opened it a crack, letting the dog in along with a cloud of dust and sand.

"Bad storm," said Lopez. "You stay, my friend. Maybe tomorrow storm be gone."

"No, the norther will be worse tomorrow," John replied. He put on his chaps and a heavy coat. "A norther usually lasts three or four days."

He pulled his hat down over his ears. Then he tied a red handkerchief over his mouth and nose.

"I'll try to get back tonight," he said picking up a pair of woolen gloves. "If I can't, I'll camp out on the range. Don't worry about me. Jed may try to make you think that something has happened to me. But you are to stay right here. Don't leave Jed alone for one minute."

"I stay, my friend."

John opened the door and stepped outside. The howling wind almost blew him against the cabin. He hurried to the horse shed, his head bent against the force of the wind.

As he slipped his saddle on his cow pony he said, "I hate to take you out in this weather. But we must see where our cattle have drifted."

John rode to the south. He knew the cattle would drift with the storm. They would look for shelter in the draws or canyons.

The dust in the air was so thick that John could see only a few yards ahead. But the wind was at his back and that helped. The little pony made good time.

After an hour's ride, John came to a wide, deep draw. He stopped on the edge and looked down. The bottom of the draw was filled with milling longhorns.

John grinned. This was fine. He had hoped to find some of the cows here, safe from the storm. As long as the wind did not bring snow or sleet the cattle would be all right.

He touched his horse lightly and rode on. He

found the rest of the herd in other sheltered places on the range. Sure that the cattle were in no danger he headed for the cabin.

It was a real battle to get back to the line cabin. Horse and rider had to face the cold, biting wind.

John leaned low in his saddle. With a gloved hand he patted his horse's neck. "Come on," he said gently. "It's tough, but we can make it."

The game little horse fought his way back over the long miles. It was almost dark, and it was getting colder every minute.

John wanted to urge his horse to greater speed. But he didn't. He knew the horse was doing his very best against the norther.

At last John saw a tiny speck of light. It was a candle burning in a window of the cabin.

When they were close to the cabin, John heard the noises of a fight going on inside. Lopez and Jed were shouting. Toby was barking.

John reined in his horse and swung from the saddle. Gun in hand he ran to the cabin.

Passing the window he caught a glimpse of

Jed and Lopez rolling on the floor. Toby was barking and biting the man.

John threw open the door.

"Jed," he ordered, "reach for the sky!"

Jed turned and looked around.

"Reach for the sky!" John said again. "Be quick about it!"

Jed let go of Lopez and rose to his feet. He raised his hands high above his head. A broken rope still hung to one wrist.

Keeping his six-shooter trained on the rustler, John kicked the door closed. He reached for a rope hanging on a peg and tossed it to Lopez.

"Tie Jed to the bunk post," he said. "I have him covered."

The Mexican boy caught the rope and scrambled to his feet. Quickly he tied Jed's arms together behind his back and then bound him to the post.

"I tie him good," said Lopez. "He no get loose again."

"How did Jed get free?" asked John.

"I go to sleep for one minute," Lopez answered in almost a whisper. "Toby bark. I wake up."

"Yes," shouted Jed. "If it hadn't been for that yapping dog, I could have escaped."

"Good old Toby!" John reached down and patted his dog's head.

"Toby big hero," praised Lopez.

"Yes, sir," John agreed. "Toby is a hero and so are you, Lopez. Believe me, you put up a good fight."

"You no angry at me?" questioned the Mexican boy.

"Angry!" exclaimed John. "I should say not! You know," he grinned, "for a couple of kids we're doing all right."

---

1. What is a line rider?

2. Describe the winter camp.

3. What are folk songs? Can you name some American folk songs?

4. Tell how John and Lopez captured Jed Dorn.

5. Here are some more cowboy words. Tell what they mean.

chaps	mustang
corral	cut out
longhorn	chuck wagon

The Golden One

THE norther lasted three more days. All the time the boys stayed in the little cabin with their prisoner. Then the wind died down, and the bright Texas sun came out again.

Lopez left the cabin to start rounding up the Bar XL cattle. The boss arrived with supplies, and left with Jed tied securely to the floor of the wagon.

"Oh, bury me not on the lone prairie!" John sang as he saddled his horse. "Come on, Toby," he called, "we're riding out to help Lopez."

Later in the day, John sighted his line partner driving a herd of longhorns to the Bar XL range. John gave his cow pony the spurs.

Lopez came galloping toward John. "What happen to bad man?" Lopez shouted to make himself heard over the bellowing of the cattle. "He escape?"

"No," John yelled in answer. He reined in his pony. "I turned Jed over to the boss," he added as the Mexican boy pulled his horse to a stop.

"What boss say?" Lopez asked. He was grinning from ear to ear.

"At first he couldn't believe that we had caught Jed Dorn."

Lopez shook with laughter. "I bet boss say we best line riders in all Texas. In world, maybe!"

"Well," John laughed, "the boss said that he was mighty proud of us."

The boys talked a while longer. Then they parted. John rode on to find another herd.

"See you tonight," he called.

"For certain, my friend," Lopez waved his big hat.

It was dark when they met at the cabin. They had driven all the cattle back on their range. Laughing and talking, they cooked supper.

"Now we can settle down to ride the line again," said John.

"I have plenty adventure," said Lopez.

The rest of the winter went by without much

more excitement. The days were spent in riding
the range. The nights were long. But there was
always plenty for the boys to do. Ropes, bridles,
and saddles had to be mended. There were books
to read, songs to sing, and plans to talk over with
each other.

John told Lopez about the handsome golden
leader of the wild herd. "I dream about that horse
every night," he sighed. "What wouldn't I give to
have him for my very own!"

"Maybe we trap the golden one," said Lopez.

"We haven't a chance."

"Someone catch him. Maybe someone who not
be good to him."

John shook his head sadly. "I hope that never
happens to the golden one."

"Then we watch for him," said Lopez. "Somehow we trap him."

All through the weeks that sped by, the boys
were on the lookout for the golden mustang. But
they never saw him or his herd of wild horses.

"We have bad luck," said Lopez. "Maybe the
golden one take his herd far away."

"I'm afraid that's what has happened," John replied. "But I won't give up looking for him. I'm sure that some day I'll find him."

Spring came. The earth turned green. It was time to drive the cattle to grazing lands nearer the ranch. The boys returned to the Bar XL to help with the spring roundup and branding.

"Boys," the boss said to them, "you'll be glad to know that Jed Dorn was sent to jail."

"Jail too good for bad man," said Lopez.

The boss laughed, then he said, "I want to do something for you boys. Would you like to have your own horses?"

"Our own horses!"

"Yes," the boss nodded. "We just came back from a wild horse roundup. You boys are each to pick the horse you like best. If you can rope and break him, he's yours!"

"Oh thanks, Boss!" exclaimed John. "Thanks a lot."

"This best luck yet," grinned Lopez.

The boys raced to the corral. They climbed up on the high gate. John drew in his breath sharply.

"Look!" he pointed to a horse in the middle of the corral. "The golden one!"

The splendid animal stood with head held high, his eyes flashing. He uttered a low, almost gentle whinny. The herd moved back and crowded against the far side of the corral.

The leader waited for the horses and colts to become quiet again. Then he snorted a warning to the two boys on the gate. He began to paw the earth with his sharp hoofs.

"You never tame him, my friend," said Lopez. "Do not try. He kill you."

"He belongs to me," John replied. "I couldn't bear to have anyone else tame him, and maybe break his spirit."

"Wait for someone to help."

"No, I'm going to do this job alone."

Rope in hand, John jumped down into the corral. His right arm circled. The rope snaked out. The loop missed the proud head, and fell limp upon the ground.

Quickly, John pulled in his rope and made the loop again. This time his aim was true. The loop circled the mustang's head and settled around his neck.

With a wild snort of anger, the mustang reared into the air. He tossed his head back and forth, trying to get rid of the rope.

John ran to a post in the corral and wound his end of the rope around it. The horse leaped forward. His sharp hoofs reached for the boy. John dodged behind the post.

The horse pulled back, trying to break the rope. But it held and the harder he pulled the more he was choked.

John hated what he was doing. But a wild horse must learn the lesson of the rope.

It seemed to John that the mustang would never give up his fight. But at last the horse stopped fighting. John edged forward and loosened the rope.

"There now, my golden one," he said in a gentle voice. "We're going to be friends."

He put his hand on the mustang's neck. A shudder ran through the animal. But he did not strike at the boy.

Quickly, John removed the rope. He ran to the gate and climbed up beside Lopez.

"He know you master," said Lopez.

John shook his head. "No, not yet. But he will learn. Isn't he a beauty?"

"Yes," the Mexican agreed. "I no want him. I take black one over there with big chest. He good to swim river. Some day I go up Texas trail. I need good swimmer to get me safe across river."

John laughed. "I hadn't thought of that."

"I break my horse first," grinned Lopez. "I ride him before the golden one let you ride him."

"I'm not going to put a saddle on Golden until he learns that he can trust me," said John. "I want him to get used to me. I want him to know the sound of my voice. I want him to know the touch of my hand."

"That take long time, my friend."

"I know. But it will be worth it."

And so the boys began to break their wild horses. In less than a week, Lopez had his horse used to the saddle. In another week he was riding the black horse around the corral. To be sure he had been thrown a few times. Few men ever broke a wild horse without "biting the dust."

John spent every free minute with Golden. As yet he had not made friends with the horse. The stubborn, proud mustang watched his would-be master with hate in his eyes.

"Are you afraid to ride your horse?" the boss asked John one day.

"Yes, I'm afraid," John admitted. "I'm scared stiff. But that won't stop me. I'll ride him when he is ready."

"When do you think that will be?"

"Well, yesterday I put my saddle on him for the first time. Today I'm going to bridle him. I'll have to wait until he is used to the bridle and saddle."

"Good luck to you, Kid."

"I'll need it," John laughed.

The day John was to ride Golden, all the cowboys were sitting on the corral fence. They were always on hand when anyone tried to ride a wild horse for the first time.

Without looking at the cowboys, John roped

Golden and bridled him. Lopez held the horse's ears while John slapped the saddle on Golden's back and quickly tightened the straps. Then he nodded to Lopez. The boy sprang away. John swung into the saddle.

Golden stood still. John was a bit surprised. Wasn't the horse going to buck? It would be easy if he didn't, but it would mean a lack of spirit.

Then, without warning, Golden exploded into action. John had been riding horses ever since he could walk. And just for the fun of it, he had ridden bucking horses whenever he had a chance. But never had he met anything like this. Golden knew more bucking tricks than all the other horses rolled into one.

For about a half dozen twisting jumps John stayed in the saddle. Then he flew through the air and landed in a heap. Glancing up he saw Golden's sharp hoofs above him. He heard the mustang squeal.

Then a loop whizzed through the air and settled around Golden's neck. The horse stopped fighting at once. John scrambled to his feet.

"Whew!" the boss exclaimed. "That's a man killer, if I ever saw one. I don't mind a good bucker, but this one is an outlaw. He can never be broken."

John's face was white. "Golden isn't an outlaw," he said. "Golden has lots of spirit, but he isn't mean. He just hates being mastered."

"I wanted that horse at first," spoke up a cowboy. "But after seeing him in action, you're welcome to him, Kid."

"Thanks."

More than ever John wanted to master the proud, stubborn Golden. He was helping to break the other wild horses for the boss. But every day, he spent at least an hour with his own mustang.

The cowboys kept telling John that he could never break an outlaw. They urged him to choose another horse.

Nothing the men said made any difference to John. Golden was the horse he wanted for his own. Quietly, gently, the boy went on trying to make Golden trust him.

At last the day came when John was ready to

ride Golden again. The horse bucked and reared and turned and twisted. But this time John sat firmly in the saddle.

Then at last Golden lowered his proud head. He had bowed to the will of his young master.

A shout went up from the watching cowboys. "Good for you, Kid!" they cheered.

John slipped from Golden's back. He wondered if those sharp hoofs would strike at him again. But this time the horse stood still.

John put his arms around Golden's neck and whispered, "We're partners now. We'll work together. Have fun together. Be friends always."

That night, the boss said to John, "You were right, Kid. Golden wasn't an outlaw. He is a mighty fine horse."

"He sure is," John agreed.

"You give boss big surprise, my friend," spoke up Lopez. "No surprise me."

The boss laughed. "I suppose you knew all the time that John could ride Golden."

"That is so," Lopez replied. "He kid yet. Yes. But he act like top hand."

Drifting

GOLDEN had lost his fight and the freedom of the range. He had lost because he was no longer afraid. The touch of a gentle hand, the sound of a gentle voice had tamed the proud, wild leader of wild horses.

John was master of his horse. But that didn't mean Golden's high spirit had been broken. Not at all! He bucked and reared and turned and twisted almost every time he was saddled.

John was glad.

"Go on and buck, you old rascal," John would laugh. "I know you're only showing off."

After a final plunging leap, Golden would settle down to the work of the day. He was learning to become a cow pony. He was learning fast, for he was smart.

In a few weeks, he could cut out a cow from the

herd with no help from John. All John had to do was to point to a cow and say, "Let's get that one!"

Golden would lay back his small, alert ears. He would weave his way through the longhorns. Then slowly, quietly he would guide the animal to the edge of the herd.

In a herd there were always some cattle the cowboys called "bunch quitters." They were the ones who kept straying from the herd.

Whenever John spotted a bunch quitter, he would touch Golden lightly. John, of course, expected his horse to race after the cow. But he had a lesson to learn.

No amount of urging would make Golden take a step. He would wait until the bunch quitter had a fair start. Then he would streak across the plain and drive the cow back to the herd.

Golden seemed to take great delight in helping his master rope. The second John roped a cow, Golden would brace himself to hold the rope tight. Sometimes he would be pulled along a few feet by the animal. But never once did the cow escape.

Before the summer was over the boss said, "Golden is the best cow pony in the outfit."

"Golden is the top cow pony in all Texas," said John. "He is mine. He is my partner."

The busy weeks on the Bar XL passed with plenty of riding and roping. Then one day, the boss told his men that he was selling out.

"The only chance to make money these days is to drive our cattle up the trail," he said. "I'm too old to make the trip, and so I'm selling out."

"We'll work for nothing until you can pay us again," spoke up John. He turned to the other cowboys. "Won't we, fellows?"

"We sure will," they agreed.

"Thanks," said the boss. "But this is my tough luck, not yours." He started walking away. Then he came back to the silent group. "Thanks for your loyalty to the outfit," he said in a choked voice. "Good luck, boys. Good luck!"

Most of the cowboys hung around while the Bar XL cattle were being sold. They hoped that the men who bought the herd would hire them to help drive the cattle up the trail. The buyers, however, had all the cowboys they needed for the drive.

"I guess I'll drift south," John said to Lopez. "Do you want to go with me?"

"I know south country," Lopez replied. "I like new country. I drift north. I no say good-by. Some day we meet again."

And this time it was John who said, "For certain, my friend. For certain."

The two shook hands warmly. Lopez mounted his black horse and rode to the north.

John called to Toby, and then swung into Golden's saddle. Boy, horse, and dog headed south.

Riding along, John thought of the day he had come to the Bar XL. The day made him think of Rusty and Packsaddle. He wondered where they were, and if he would ever see them again.

"I owe a lot to them," he told Golden. "Rusty, of course, is my best friend. He gave me my first job. I was only a dogie then."

John laughed softly to himself. "I'm not a real cowboy yet. There are many things I need to know. I'll drift around for a few years, learning

what I can at other ranches. But some day I'll
have my own ranch—some day."

And during the next six years, John drifted
over a large part of Texas. He worked at many
ranches. Everyone he worked for said that he was
a top hand. A boss could depend upon him. He
was honest. He was loyal to the outfit.

At every ranch where John worked the cowboys
wanted to buy Golden. But John refused to sell
his proud, handsome horse. His answer was
always the same.

"No amount of money can buy Golden," he said.
"We're partners, Golden and I. We're riding the
range together."

"Well, all right," the cowboy would reply. "I
don't blame you. But if you ever change your
mind, let me know."

"I'll remember," John would laugh. Then to
Golden he would say, "Don't worry. I'll never sell
you, my beauty."

Shortly after his twenty-first birthday, John
went to work for Charles Wulfjen. His cowboys
called him "Boss Charlie." He had a ranch

in Texas and one in the Wyoming Territory.

"I'm planning to drive a herd of cattle up to my ranch in Wyoming," Boss Charlie told John. "Have you been up the trail?"

"No," John replied. "I have always wanted to make the trip. But I haven't been lucky, I guess."

"Lucky! You may change your mind about that. The trail drive is a buster."

"I know," John smiled. "I have heard men talk for hours about the work, hardships, and dangers. But they all love the trail."

"You're right, there," the boss laughed. "It is adventure—real adventure to ride the long trail."

At first John was just another cowboy on the new ranch. In a short time, however, Boss Charlie came to depend upon him more and more.

One day John was asked to have supper at the ranch house. He met Mrs. Wulfjen and the two little Wulfjen girls.

The younger daughter's name was Eula. She was five years old. She was a fairy-like child. Her hair was the color of sunlight and she had big brown eyes.

All during the evening Eula kept watching John. At last she went over to him and said, "I like you. When I grow up, I'm going to marry you."

Everyone laughed.

"Girls, it's time for bed," their gentle mother said.

Eula walked to the door. She turned and looked at John. "Don't forget, I am going to marry you."

John smiled at the little girl. "All right, Eula," he said. "I'll remember."

The girls and their mother left the room. The two men settled down to talk about the trail drive.

"When are we going to hit the trail?" John asked.

"We're leaving the ranch in a few days," Boss Charlie answered. "We're heading for the bay section in southeast Texas. We'll round up our herd there, and then hit the long trail to the north."

"How big a herd do you plan to buy?"

"Oh, about thirty-five hundred head of cattle."

John whistled. "That's a lot of cows for ten cowboys to handle."

"All my men, except you, have been up the trail. They know their business. But I always start out with a few extra cowboys. Somewhere along the way we're bound to run into tough luck. So while I was in Austin the other day, I hired two more men to help with the drive."

"Have they been up the trail?"

"Yes," the boss replied, "and they know the Wyoming country, too. They have worked up north for several years. But they were homesick for Texas. They came back to spend the winter."

John, glancing out a window, saw two men riding toward the horse corral. "I guess your men are here," he said.

The boss rose to his feet and walked to the door. "Howdy, boys," he called.

"Howdy, Boss!" came the answer. "Howdy!"

John sat up straight in his chair. Then he grabbed his hat. With quick long strides he hurried to the door and rushed outside.

"Rusty!" he shouted. "Packsaddle!"

The two men turned in their saddles. "John!" they exclaimed. "John!"

They reined in their horses and swung to the ground. John ran to meet them.

Laughing, talking, the good friends shook hands. Their noisy good humor brought Toby racing from the bunk house.

"This is like old times," said Rusty patting the dog. "Say there, Toby, don't knock me down."

John laughed. "Toby is almost as glad as I am to see you and Packsaddle."

"Say, John," asked Packsaddle, "are you going up the trail with us?"

"Yes, I am. It's my first trail drive."

"Yipee!" Packsaddle let out a loud cheer. "Yipee!"

Rusty asked, "What have you been doing, John?"

"Well, I stayed at the Bar XL until the boss sold out. The rest of the time I have drifted around. I haven't worked here very long."

"Is it a good outfit?"

"The best!" John exclaimed. "The boys are a good bunch of fellows. And Boss Charlie is a top hand."

"Do you still want to have your own ranch?"
John nodded.

"And the long rope?" questioned Rusty. "Have
you changed your mind about that?"

"No," John answered quickly. "I'll never throw
the long rope, Rusty. Never!"

"That's all I want to know."

Rusty looked John over carefully. The years
had changed the boy into a tall, handsome young
man.

Everything about John told of his active outdoor
life on the range. Wind and sun had tanned his
skin. Long trails had made his gray eyes steady
and keen. He had the slightly-swaying gait of a
man who rode more than he walked. From the
crown of his ten-gallon hat to the soles of his
high-heeled boots, he was all cowboy.

Packsaddle turned to Rusty. "The kid is all
right."

Rusty's blue eyes began to twinkle. A smile
pulled at the corners of his mouth.

"John isn't a kid any longer," he said. "We're
going up the trail with John Kendrick, Cowboy."

Texas Longhorns

THE roundup at the bay was like the others in which John had taken part. The cowboys rounded up and branded thirty-five hundred cattle. All the longhorns were marked with Boss Charlie's WJ brand. The long, long trail drive was about to begin.

John had not been up the trail. But he knew each cowboy had certain duties to perform. Each man cared for the horses in his string. Each man was given a special riding position.

The two most experienced men, of course, would lead the herd. They were called the "point riders."

The other men would follow at regular spaces to keep the cattle in line. The two least experienced men or the two youngest men in the outfit, would ride in the rear of the herd.

All cowboys hated to ride the rear position. It

was the worst job on the trail. The cattle in the rear were the ones that could not keep up with the herd. They were the "drags," as the cowboys called them. Some were lame or weak. Others were just plain lazy and stubborn.

Besides having trouble with the cattle, the rear riders had to put up with the dust of the trail. A moving herd kicked up great clouds of blinding, choking dust. Small wonder the cowboys hated to ride the drag position.

Boss Charlie's cowboys hated the drag position, too. The last night in camp they waited to learn their riding positions.

"I guess I'm the only one who doesn't have to worry," said John. "I know I'll end up as a drag rider."

"Yes," Rusty agreed. "You're the youngest man in the outfit."

"And I'm the next youngest," said Mac, a lean, suntanned cowboy. He turned to John. "We'll eat plenty of dust for the next six months."

"Sure," John laughed. "But we'll make it all right."

"Who will be the point riders?" asked a cowboy.

"Rusty will be one," spoke up Packsaddle. "I'll be riding right behind him."

"You seem pretty sure of it," said the cowboy. "Did the boss tell you?"

"No," Packsaddle replied. "But that's the way it will be. Rusty has always been top hand in the outfits where we have worked. He leads and I follow."

"Here comes the boss," said a cowboy. "He will tell us our riding positions."

The boss strode to the campfire. "Boys," he said, "I'm giving my orders tonight. It will save time. In the morning we hit the trail."

He paused and looked around the circle of silent cowboys. "Our herd is a big one," he went on. "The cattle are as wild as jack rabbits. We'll have plenty of trouble with them until they are used to the trail. The best thing to do is to drive them hard for the first few days. It will be tough on you boys. I'm sorry, but it can't be helped. On the trail, the cattle come first—last—and always."

The men nodded. All the way up the trail the cattle and horses would be given special care. Everything would be done to keep the animals in good shape.

But a cowboy could expect no such care. If he became ill or was hurt, there was just one of two things he could do. He could get well or die. In either case the quicker the better. Nothing must interfere with the cattle drive.

"Keep the herd moving," was the law of the trail. It was a stern law. But it was obeyed by the riding, roping cowboys of the old cattle trails. Keep the herd moving!

The boss went on with his orders. The men were told their riding positions.

John, much to his surprise, was not made a drag rider along with Mac. Instead John was given the second position in Rusty's line. The first position was given to Packsaddle.

"I guess that's all," the boss said as he finished. "Turn in early tonight." He left to talk to the cook of the outfit.

"The boss must think you're pretty good," Mac

said to John. "You're right up in front with the top hands."

"I know," John replied. "I'll have to do some fancy riding to keep up with them."

"Well, I don't need to worry about that. The drags won't mind how I ride."

"I'm sorry, fellow," said John. "It's tough luck."

"It could be worse," Mac grinned. "The boss might have left me at the ranch."

"I wish he had left me at the ranch," said the other drag rider. "I'd like to quit right now."

"Why don't you?" Packsaddle asked. "John's dog can take your place."

The cowboy snorted and walked away.

"Come on, men," Rusty yawned. "Let's hit the hay."

In a few minutes, the camp was quiet. John, lying on the ground, looked up at the bright stars. Although he was tired, he could not go to sleep. He kept thinking of the drive and wondering what adventures he would find along the trail. At last he fell asleep.

John thought he had been asleep only a short

time when he was awakened by a loud shout. It was, however, almost daylight. The cook was calling, "Come and get it! Come and get it or I'll throw it out!"

Sleepy men rolled out of their blankets. "All right!" they grumbled. "We're coming."

Breakfast was eaten in a hurry. The horses of the outfit were driven into camp. Each cowboy roped a horse from his string. Then two men started up the trail with the extra horses.

"Well, boys," said Boss Charlie, "this is it. We're heading for my ranch in Wyoming. It's a long, long drive of fifteen hundred miles."

John studied the faces of the cowboys. Their usual smiles were gone. They were sober now. All knew the chances they were taking. All knew the dangers. And yet all loved the long trail with its daring, reckless adventures.

"We're ready, Boss," said Rusty.

"Good!" The boss mounted his horse. "Come on, men, let's ride."

With a cheer the cowboys raced to their riding positions. Whooping and hollering, they tried to get the cattle started and headed up the trail.

At first, the longhorns wanted to go everywhere but north. It was all the cowboys could do to keep them from stampeding.

Boss Charlie rode up and down the lines giving orders to his men. He pulled his horse to a stop beside John. "The cattle haven't picked a leader," he said. "Until they do, we are in for plenty of trouble."

"Maybe I can pick a leader for them," John grinned.

He stood up in his stirrups and looked over the milling herd. He pointed to a longhorn. "Maybe that one is a leader. Shall I cut him out and drive him ahead?"

"Do you want to risk that handsome horse of yours among all those horns?"

"Don't worry about Golden," John patted his horse's neck. "Come on, old fellow, let's get him."

Golden laid back his ears and headed for the cow. Carefully the horse wove his way through the herd. Twisting and turning, he dodged the long, sharp horns. At last he reached the cow

John had chosen for a leader of the trail herd.

"Good boy," praised John. "Cut him out."

Golden gave the cow a gentle push. Then slowly he guided the animal to the edge of the herd.

"You're good, John," said the boss. "That was as pretty a job of cutting out as I have ever seen."

"Thanks, but I didn't have a thing to do with it," John replied. "Golden knows all the tricks."

Boss Charlie and John drove the longhorn to the head of the herd. At first the cattle took no notice of the chosen leader. But when he started up the trail a few longhorns began to follow. Then more and more fell in line. At last they were all following the leader.

The boss gave a sigh of relief. "Keep the herd moving!" he shouted to Rusty. "Keep the herd moving!"

Rusty's answer was drowned out by the clashing of horns. But he waved his big hat to signal that he understood the order.

"All right, John," said the boss. "Get back to your line position."

John touched Golden lightly.

Golden raced past Rusty and Packsaddle. He sped on to a spot halfway between Packsaddle and the next rider. And then without any signal from John the horse swung into line.

John threw back his head and laughed. "You old rascal!" He leaned forward in the saddle and patted Golden's neck.

"This is the long trail I have told you about. Remember?" John asked. "This is the trail of adventure. We're riding it together, partner. Let's have a good time!"

---

1. How did John train Golden to become a good cow pony?

2. What lesson did Golden teach John?

3. What did John do after he left the Bar XL?

4. Tell how John meets Rusty and Packsaddle again?

5. What was the law of the trail?

6. Why were the best cowboys chosen to be "point riders?"

7. Why didn't the men like to ride the "drag position?"

8. Tell how John helped get the herd started up the trail.

The Chisholm Trail

THE cowboys kept the herd on the move. At first, the men enjoyed the excitement of the drive. After four days and three nights of hard riding, it was another story. They were nearly dead from lack of food and sleep.

True, they had taken turns to grab something to eat and to snatch a few hours rest. And they were old hands at dozing in their saddles as they rode along. But long hours on the trail had stamped deep lines of weariness into their faces.

They were too tired to sit straight. When they dismounted to change horses, they staggered, almost falling in their tracks.

At sunset on the fourth day, Boss Charlie ordered a halt. Weary cowboys drove the cattle off the trail to let them graze until dusk.

John, like the other men, slouched in his saddle

as he watched the herd. And like the others, he kept an eye on the cook in camp.

John asked himself, "What's the matter with that old woman tonight? Isn't he ever going to have supper ready?"

At last, the cook sang out the old call, "Come and get it, boys."

Rusty and the cowboys in his line raced to camp. The rest stayed with the cattle.

As John swung to the ground Toby came bounding to him. Wearily, John reached down and patted the dog's head.

"Hello, old fellow," he said. "How do you like riding with the cook on this trip?"

The cook was standing a few feet away. He began to laugh.

"You have it all wrong, John," he said. "On this trip I'm riding with Toby. That dog thinks my chuck wagon belongs to him."

"I hope Toby doesn't make any trouble for you."

"Trouble! Why, we have fine times together."

After the men ate supper, they mounted fresh horses and rode back to the herd. The other cowboys went in to eat. In half an hour or so, they returned with the boss. They also were mounted on fresh horses.

"Boys," ordered the boss, "round up the cattle. It's time they were bedded down for the night."

The cowboys formed a big ring around the herd. Then they started riding round and round the longhorns. Slowly the herd was crowded into a tight, close circle.

When the herd was quiet, two men took over the first stretch of guard duty. The rest of the cowboys returned to camp.

They cared for the horses in their strings. Then each man bridled and saddled a horse to have ready in case of trouble.

Some of the men kept their cow ponies near camp. Others took their horses into camp and fell asleep holding the long bridle reins in their hands. Each cowboy picked the best pony in his string for night work. Usually this horse was ridden only at night. Besides being a good-all-around cow pony, the horse was gentle, sure-footed, and keen of sight.

John, of course, chose Golden for his night horse. Several times John was awakened by a touch on his shoulder. It was Golden pressing his soft, velvety nose against his master. The faithful horse was telling John that all was well in camp and with the herd.

The night passed all too quickly. At daylight, the men awakened. Another day of work began.

While the men ate breakfast, the boss said, "The cattle are out of their old range country. Now we can settle down to the daily drive of ten to fifteen miles."

"Yes," grinned Rusty. "The rest is easy, fellows. We only have to worry about stampedes, storms, river crossings, and quicksand."

The men laughed, and so did Boss Charlie.

"Well," he said, "I'll ride on to find water for the herd."

Shortly after the boss left camp, the cowboys were in their saddles. Laughing and talking, they rode to their herd positions.

The cattle were grazing. The cowboys let them graze, but kept them moving slowly up the trail.

Sometime about eight o'clock, the chuck wagon flew by with a great clatter of pots and pans. John caught a glimpse of Toby on the high seat beside the cook.

"That dog will be as spoiled as a cowboy," John laughed to himself. "I've never known a cowboy to walk anywhere, if he can ride."

When the herd had grazed two or three miles, it was guided back to the trail. The cattle milled around to find their usual places.

The cowboys waited for the leader to take his place and for the drags to fall behind. At last the longhorns were in order.

"Hi! Yi!" the cowboys shouted. "Hi! Yi!"

The great herd swung into motion. Horns clashed. Dust rose in thick clouds. Cattle bellowed. Cowboys shouted.

About four miles up the trail, the boss and the cook were waiting. The boss had found water for the herd.

After the cattle had been watered, they laid down to rest during the heat of the day. The cowboys also had a chance to rest. They ate their

noonday meal, and then changed to fresh horses.

Late in the afternoon, the cattle were rounded up again. They were driven seven or eight more miles up the trail. Then they were turned out to graze until they were bedded down for the night.

"Well, John, what do you think of the drive?" Rusty asked that night.

"It's great," John answered.

"It's a good thing you like it," laughed Pack-saddle. "Because this is what we will do day after day after day."

"That's all right with me," John replied with a grin.

And day after day, the cattle drive was the same. Near Austin, the men started up the real trail—the Chisholm Trail. This was the most famous cattle trail in all the West.

Part of the trail had been laid out in 1865 by Jesse Chisholm, a half-breed Cherokee Indian. He had been a scout and trader. His trade wagon had cut the first ruts into the trail. Now the trail was a wide, bare, dusty highway. Like a great brown ribbon, it stretched six hundred miles from

Texas on up to the cow towns of Kansas.

The cowboys loved the old Chisholm Trail. Seldom did they gather around their campfires without singing a few stanzas of their favorite song.

> "Come along my boys
> And listen to my tale,
> All about my troubles
> On the Old Chisholm Trail.
>
> Oh, I started up the trail
> October twenty-third.
> Oh, I started up the trail
> With a 2 U herd."

And one day like the old song, Boss Charlie and his boys had trouble with their herd. The day was hot, with scarcely a breath of air. The cattle lagged. The cowboys had to whoop and holler to keep them moving.

Late in the afternoon, dark clouds gathered. The setting sun glowed an angry red. After supper, a cold wind began to blow.

Boss Charlie left camp and rode out to the

bedding ground. In a short time he returned. There was a worried look on his tired face.

"What's the matter, Boss?" the cowboys asked.

"The cattle are restless," the boss shook his head. "They are milling around and won't bed down."

"Who are on guard?" asked a man.

"Rusty and Packsaddle."

"Maybe we better ride out to the herd," said the man.

"No," Boss Charlie replied. "That won't be necessary. But I'll double the guard. John, you and Mac get out there. The rest of you men sleep with your boots on. I have a hunch there will be a stampede tonight."

John and Mac swung into their saddles and raced from camp. When they neared the bedding ground, Rusty called, "That you, John?"

"Yes," John answered. "Mac is with me."

"Good!" Rusty rode on singing. His voice was exactly like him—big, strong, and friendly.

Just then a rumble of thunder came from the east. A zigzag of lightning split the sky. Thunder rolled nearer and nearer. Darkness fell like a black curtain. A blast of cold air blew in, followed by an icy drive of rain.

Lightning cracked close at hand. In the flash of light, John saw the boss and the cowboys come riding out of camp.

"Keep the cattle milling to the left!" the boss shouted. "And sing, men, sing!"

"Oh, bury me not on the lone prairie," John sang at the top of his lungs. The meaning of the words hit him with full force. This was the lone prairie all right. Well he knew that Death might be riding at his side tonight.

Then came another flash of lightning and the worst crash of thunder yet. The cattle were off in a wild stampede.

John was caught right in front of the herd. The roar of pounding hoofs was in his ears. He could feel the hot breath of the racing animals. Horns grazed his arms. He let Golden feel the spurs.

He leaned forward in his saddle. "Get us out of this, fellow," he pleaded. "Get us out of this!"

John knew the dangers that lay in their path.

Deep gullies cut the land. Even in daylight when a rider could see, there was danger.

If Golden should step in a prairie dog hole! John shuddered at the thought. If he were thrown from his horse, he didn't have a chance. He would be ground to pulp beneath the pounding hoofs of the longhorns.

After what seemed hours, John was ahead of the cattle. He guided Golden to one side and worked to turn the herd. Other men were working with him. At last the herd began to circle.

The men started singing again. The stampede was over. The thunder and lightning stopped. The rain came down more gently. The herd quieted.

Weary men returned to camp. The cook had steaks, brown biscuits, and a pot of steaming coffee ready.

"I'm so hungry I could eat my boots," John said. He piled his plate high with food and sat on his heels to eat.

Then he looked up. The other men looked up at the same time. They looked at one another. Each put down his plate without touching a bite.

There came Rusty's horse, the saddle twisted to one side.

John jumped to his feet. "Has anyone seen Rusty?"

No one answered.

"Come on, boys!" Boss Charlie was already on his horse.

Without a word, the men mounted their horses. They rode out to where the cattle had stampeded. Before long Mac went back to camp to get a shovel.

What was left of poor Rusty was lowered into a grave. The men took off their hats and bowed their heads. The boss prayed briefly.

Quietly the men returned to camp, leaving Packsaddle and John standing beside the new grave. Not far away the cattle had bedded down for the night. The guards were singing,

> "Come along my boys
> And listen to my tale,
> All about my troubles
> On the Old Chisholm Trail."

Red River Crossing

PACKSADDLE and John knelt beside the grave. Neither spoke.

At last, Packsaddle rose slowly to his feet. He stumbled through the darkness to his horse.

John stood up and hurried to Golden. His hands trembled as he took the bridle reins and swung into the saddle.

The two men headed for camp. As they rode along John said, "I'll always remember Rusty. He was my best friend, and I never knew his real name."

"I didn't know Rusty's real name either," said Packsaddle. "Come to think of it, I never told him mine. We were friends for more than twenty years.

"I guess we always had more important things to talk about than who we were and where we used to live. Now Rusty is gone. The old trail and the range will never be the same to me again."

Packsaddle's voice broke. Then he added, "The Big Boss in the Sky sure picked a top hand tonight."

Silently they rode to camp—to sleep if they could. The drive must go on!

And day after day, the great herd pushed on up the Chisholm Trail. Spring, too, with all its beauty was moving north.

Green grass stretched for miles across the gently rolling country. Bluebonnets and other bright wild flowers bloomed everywhere. John was sure that no place on earth could be as beautiful as Texas in the spring.

The cowboys kept the herd moving. There were creeks and rivers on the trail. There were no bridges across the streams.

The Colorado River was the first real river the cowboys had to cross. To make the crossing, the herd was divided into bunches of about five hundred head of cattle.

The cowboys had a little trouble driving the

first bunch into the river. But at last the leader started across, and the rest followed.

Shouting and yelling, the cowboys guided the cows to the other bank. Then, as the cattle scrambled up the bank, the cowboys rode back to drive another bunch across the river. Several hours later, the whole herd was across.

Now it was the cook's turn to drive his chuck wagon across the river. Toby was up on the high front seat beside the cook. As the cook cracked his long whip Toby barked with delight. The horses plunged into the water. Two cowboys rode on each side of the wagon to keep it from tipping over into the stream.

"Well," John said when the crossing was finished, "that wasn't too bad. I expected to do a little swimming."

"Wait until we come to the Red River," spoke up a cowboy. "If you're looking for a swim, you'll get it there."

"You boys are doing all right," said Boss Charlie. "But let me say again. Get this herd through in good shape. I guess you all know that every boss has a standing offer with his men. If they make the drive without a stampede, every man in the outfit gets a new suit of clothes."

"I reckon that offer won't do us much good," grinned Mac. "We have had one stampede already."

"I have never heard of an outfit making the trip without a stampede," said another cowboy. "I don't think it can be done. Do you, Boss?"

"No," Boss Charlie admitted with a slow smile. "So far we have been lucky, except for our pal Rusty. But I can't help wishing that we were on the other side of the Red."

"I wish we were, too," said Packsaddle. "It's one river crossing that really is tough."

Days later, the men neared the Red River. The trail was rougher, but it was easy to follow. Years of use had cut a wide, deep path into the red soil.

The cowboys had a feeling that they were headed for more trouble. A cloudy sky added to their worry. At best, the Red would not be easy to cross. But after a rain, it would be even more difficult.

The men kept watching the gray sky. In the

afternoon, it began to rain. At first, it was only a light shower. Then the rain poured down.

The boss ordered a halt. The men tried to bed down the herd. But the cattle kept milling around. It was all the cowboys could do to keep them from stampeding.

Somehow the cook managed to get a hot supper ready. Two men at a time came in to eat. When they had eaten they hurried back to the cattle.

All night it rained. All night the cattle milled, bawled, and refused to bed down. All night the cowboys were in their saddles. All night they circled the herd, singing until they were hoarse.

In the early morning the storm ended. Weary men rode into camp for breakfast. They huddled around the campfire trying to dry their wet clothes.

"How about it, Boss?" asked Mac. "Will we cross the Red today?"

"No," Boss Charlie answered. "After all this rain, the river is at flood stage. We'll have to wait until the water goes down to a safer level. You boys can take it easy today."

The day was spent in camp. The men took turns watching the herd. When their hours of guard duty were over, some fell asleep. Others went to the little supply store near by.

John and Packsaddle rode out following the trail to the river. John thought he had never seen a meaner, uglier river than the old Red. How could they ever drive the herd across this raging, mile-wide stream? The muddy waters whirled by, tossing trunks of trees about as though they were leaves.

"No wonder you boys wish we were over the Red," said John. "I do, too, now that I have had a good look at it."

Packsaddle laughed. "I remember I was scared stiff the first time I crossed it. That was years ago. I had just met Rusty. We were going up the trail together for the first time."

He sighed and then began to talk about the river again. "The Red is the boundary line between Texas and the Indian country. In the old days we had plenty of trouble with the redskins. Now they are more peaceful. But they are always out to get a few 'Whoa Haws,' if they can."

"Whoa Haws?" questioned John.

"That's the Indian name for cattle," Packsaddle explained. "It all started when white men used oxen to haul their wagons across the plains. Oxen, you know, are not driven with reins like horses. Instead they are guided by shouted commands. When the men wanted the oxen to stop, they called, 'Whoa.' And 'Haw' means to turn toward the driver. From these two orders the Indians began to call oxen 'Whoa Haws.' Now it's their name for all cattle."

John looked across the river to the Indian country. He wondered what adventures were waiting there for him.

"Let's ride to the store," said Packsaddle.

"Sure," John replied. He touched his horse lightly.

The store was hardly more than a shack. But stores were far apart on the western trails. And so the owner did a lively business.

"Yes, sir," the owner boasted to Boss Charlie's men, "every outfit stops at my store. I carry everything from cowboy shirts to dried apples."

"Dried apples!" The cowboys turned to their cook.

"All right," the cook laughed. "I'll take some dried apples, too. And I'll build you fellows some apple pies for supper."

After the cook left, the owner waited on the cowboys. "I have the best stock of clothes on the trail," he said. "Yes, sir, I have everything. I have shirts, socks, chaps, jeans, hats—everything. Six-shooters and ammunition, too. Yes, sir, boys, I have everything."

The cowboys bought the clothes they needed. As they started back to camp the owner asked, "Where are you fellows going?"

"We're headed for Wyoming," answered Packsaddle. "The boss has a ranch up there."

"Wyoming is getting to be quite a cow country," said the store keeper. "I keep pretty well posted on trail drives you know. And every year more outfits are driving their herds up to Wyoming. It must be a great country."

"It is," Packsaddle replied.

"Good luck!" the owner called as the cowboys raced back to camp.

John thought of the Red River. "We'll need plenty of luck," he said to himself. "We sure will."

That night the men had apple pie for supper. Later, they gathered around the campfire to sing their favorite songs. Why worry about tomorrow and the Red River crossing!

"Let's sing 'The Dying Cowboy,'" said Mac as he tuned his old fiddle.

"What! Again!" Packsaddle exclaimed. "Don't you ever get tired of that song?"

Mac grinned. "All right, then you name it."

"My favorite song is 'Forty Years a Cow Puncher,'" said Packsaddle. "Let's sing it, boys."

Mac struck up the tune, and the men began to sing. For more than an hour they stayed at the campfire, singing one song after another. Then they spread their blankets on the ground, and went to sleep.

At sunrise, the men were up and ready for the day's work. While they ate breakfast, the boss gave his orders.

"The Red is too wide for us to cross with bunches of cattle," he said. "Our horses couldn't stand the strain of swimming back and forth. I guess we couldn't do it either. So we are driving the whole herd across at one time."

The cowboys nodded.

The boss went on, "You all know what to do. Get the cattle into the water and then keep them going. Don't let them drift down the river with the current. Above all don't let them start milling. If they do, we may lose the entire herd."

"We'll do our best," the men said.

"Good! Let's go!"

The cowboys swung into their saddles. "Hi! Yi!" they shouted. They rounded up the herd and started for the river.

"All right, fellows," Boss Charlie shouted. "It's every man for himself now. You are on your own."

The boss raced on ahead. Bellowing cattle followed the wide trail down the steep, red bank. Yelling cowboys rode along driving the cattle out into the swift current of the river.

As John started into the river, he saw a great tree trunk coming down the stream. It was directly in the path of the cattle. If the cattle were hit, then they would start milling.

John shouted a warning. But his voice could not carry above the bawling of the herd. Filled with horror, he closed his eyes for a second.

And then it happened. The tree hit the cattle. At once the animals began to mill.

John gave Golden the spurs. The horse plunged into the water and headed toward the whirling mass of long, sharp horns.

The cowboys snapped into action. They worked to stop the milling of the crazy, mad herd. They yelled and fired their six-shooters into the air. They beat the animals with their whips.

At last, the mill was broken. The cattle began to head toward the other bank of the river.

John and the men tried to keep the herd from drifting down the river. The cattle in the lead reached shore. They scrambled up the high bank and fell to the ground. They were too tired to stampede.

The cowboys and their horses were no less tired. But their work would not be over until the whole herd was safely across.

John watched Golden closely. He did not want his horse to become too tired. They were still far from shore when John slipped from Golden's back.

"I'll swim the rest of the way," said John. He caught hold of his horse's mane and began to swim along with Golden.

John looked around and saw the other cowboys were swimming beside their mounts. Like John, the men had chosen the best horses in their strings for the river crossing. And each man would rather swim than let his favorite horse do all the work. Bobbing along with Golden, John reached the shore. Golden shook his sturdy body and the muddy water flew every way.

"Say, there," John laughed as he mounted. "I'm wet enough without your trying to drown me."

Golden climbed up on the high bank with the cattle. John rode out to help Boss Charlie and another cowboy guard the resting herd.

Wearily, John slumped in his saddle and looked

around. A riderless horse came tearing up the bank with the longhorns.

"Packsaddle!" cried John. "That's Pack-saddle's horse!"

John raced to the bank of the river. He looked for Packsaddle among the cowboys swimming along with the rest of the herd. He did not see his friend.

On the other side, the cook was waiting with his chuck wagon. Some men were building a raft to bring the chuck wagon across the river. Two cowboys were swimming the extra horses of the outfit across.

"Maybe Packsaddle is with them," John thought. But when the men came ashore with the extra horses, Packsaddle was not with them. Nor was he with the group who came across with the chuck wagon.

Sick at heart John watched the muddy Red River. On the bank where he stood he counted six graves.

Packsaddle wouldn't even have a grave along the trail he loved. His body had been carried away by the swift, raging current of the river.

John went back to camp. The men were quiet. They tried to tell John that they would miss Packsaddle, too. They didn't say much, but then they never did when they were sad.

Words couldn't bring Packsaddle back again. So what good did it do to talk about his death. A cowboy learned to keep his sorrow to himself.

Supper was eaten almost in silence. Later, the men gathered around their campfire.

Mac brought out his fiddle. John hoped the men wouldn't sing "The Dying Cowboy" tonight.

They didn't. Mac looked at John and then at the others in the circle.

"Let's sing one song," he said. "Let's sing 'Forty Years a Cow Puncher' in honor of our friend who isn't with us tonight."

The song was Packsaddle's funeral service.

Whoa Haws and Barbed Wire

THE drive must go on! The words kept pounding in John's mind. No matter what happens, the drive must go on.

In the morning at the usual hour, John was in his saddle. He rode to the river.

"Good-by, Packsaddle," he said quietly. "You didn't have to cross the Red without Rusty after all."

Somehow the thought brought a little comfort to John. He turned his horse around and rode back to the herd.

The cowboys had already taken their line positions. Boss Charlie was in the lead.

"Say, John," he called, "come here."

John raced forward. As he reined in his horse he asked, "Anything wrong?"

"No," the boss replied. "I just want you to

150

help me count the herd. I must find out how many cows we lost in the river crossing yesterday."

John nodded.

"By the way," the boss said, "Packsaddle's point riding position is yours—if you want it. Do you?"

"It was Rusty's old position, too," said John. He hesitated a second and then added, "Thanks, Boss, I'd like to take over for both of them."

"I thought you would. Good luck to you, John. Now let's count the herd."

Boss Charlie rode to the other side of the cattle. He called in a loud voice, "All right, boys, we're ready."

The cowboys let the herd stretch out in a long line. Then the men drove the cattle slowly up the trail between John and the boss.

John had a saddle string in his hand. When he had counted one hundred cows he tied a knot in the string. Then he began counting again: one, two, three, four, and so on up to a hundred. For every one hundred cows he counted he tied another knot in the string.

Boss Charlie, on his side of the herd, was doing the same. When the count was over the two men checked their scores. Each had thirty-four knots in his string and had counted up to eighty again.

"Well," said the boss, "that means twenty cows were drowned yesterday."

"I'm surprised we didn't lose more," said John.

"So am I. We might have lost the whole herd. But you boys are a good outfit."

The boss rode on to find a camp site. The cowboys kept the herd moving slowly up the trail. For miles ahead the great trail cut almost straight north through the Indian country.

Already some white men had settled in the Indian country. They, of course, had no right to the land. It belonged to the Indians.

Later the Indian country became a part of the state of Oklahoma. And today it is a rich section of ranch and farm lands.

But in 1879 it was a wild, rugged country. And John on his first trip up the trail, kept looking for Indians.

One day without warning, five mounted Indian braves swept down a hill. Their feathered war-bonnets streamed out in the wind. Yelling and kicking the sides of their ponies, they raced toward the grazing herd.

"Get the cattle on the trail!" Boss Charlie shouted to his cowboys. "John! Mac! Come with me."

The three men rode out to meet the Indians. When they were near, the brave wearing the biggest warbonnet held up his right hand. At once, the other Indians reined in their ponies.

The Indian came on alone. "Me big chief," he said pulling his pony to a quick stop.

"I am a big chief, too," Boss Charlie replied.

"This land belong to Indian," the chief scowled. "Indian no like Whoa Haws on trail. White men chase buffalo away. Turn back."

"No," Boss Charlie patted the six-shooter in his belt. "We will not turn back. But we will not make trouble for you. We only want to pass through your country."

"No pass! Turn back!"

Boss Charlie refused. He shook his head.

The chief raised his hand. At the signal, thirty or more Indians came tearing down the hill.

While the Indians held a powwow, John took a quick look around. The cowboys had the cattle on the trail and were driving them along at a lively pace.

"What are we going to do, Boss?" asked Mac. "We can't fight all these Indians."

"We may have to fight. We're not turning back."

John admired Boss Charlie's cool courage. But maybe the boss was being too daring. And yet what else was there to do? They couldn't turn back now.

John watched the Indian powwow. Over and over the chief kept saying something about Whoa Haws. Each time the braves nodded their heads. At last the chief left the band and raced straight to Boss Charlie.

"My people hungry," the chief said. "You give many Whoa Haws. We no fight."

Boss Charlie smiled with relief. "You are a

wise chief," he said. He held up three fingers.

"No," the chief held up both hands. He opened and closed them many times. Each time meant that he wanted ten cattle for letting the herd pass through his land.

The boss shook his head. "Three," he said. Again he held up three fingers.

The chief raised his hands and opened and closed them several times.

Boss Charlie merely shook his head.

The chief held up his hands again. This time he was ready to settle for ten Whoa Haws.

The boss held up three fingers.

The chief held up just one hand.

Boss Charlie nodded. He turned to John and Mac. "Cut out five drags. Get going before this Indian changes his mind."

The cowboys raced to the herd. They cut out five drags and drove them back to the Indians. At once the yelling braves began to chase the bawling longhorns across the plains.

"Look at those cows run!" Mac laughed.

The boss grinned. "If a bunch of Indians were

chasing me, I think I could run that fast, too."

"That was a close call, Boss," said John. "I thought for awhile we really would have to fight."

"So did I," Boss Charlie replied. "But we didn't. Let's hit the trail."

Day after day the drive went on. The trail led ever to the north. The men were now in a dry part of the country. Streams and water holes were far apart.

One morning the boss could not find water for the herd. The men had water to drink. The cook always kept a barrel of water tied to a side of his chuck wagon. But the cattle had no water.

Hoping to find water for the herd, the men pushed on up the trail. Darkness came, and still the boss had not found a water hole.

Camp was made. The night guard was doubled, as the thirsty cattle would not bed down. All night long the cattle bawled for water.

It was hard to get the cattle started in the morning. Time and again they tried to stray from the trail. It was all the cowboys could do to keep the herd moving.

"We're in for trouble," Boss Charlie told his men. "If a breeze comes up from the south, the cattle will be sure to smell water. And then all the cowboys in Texas couldn't keep them from turning back."

Shortly before noon a gust of hot wind blew up from the south. With the wind came the smell of water.

For a minute the great herd stood still. The drags turned first. Then, with their tails in the air and their long horns clashing, they thundered south. In only a few minutes every animal in the herd was racing back over the trail.

The cowboys tried to stop them. But Boss Charlie had been right. All the cowboys in Texas could not have held them now.

"Let them go, boys!" the boss shouted. "Let them go! Save your horses!"

The cattle were crazy with thirst. They stampeded back to the last place where they had been watered. The men followed in dust clouds that hung in the air long after the herd had passed.

In the morning, the men rounded up the herd.
The cattle were allowed to drink their fill before
heading north again.

All day the cowboys kept the herd moving.
Long after dark camp was made. But even then,
the cowboys had no chance to sleep. They were
on guard duty all night. Before sunrise they had
the herd on the trail again.

Somehow the day passed. The long hours of
the night dragged on to another day of scorching
heat.

In spite of the heat, John was cold. He shivered
as he took his place in line. He hoped he was not
going to be ill.

He looked ahead. The trail stretched for endless
miles across the treeless country. There was
nothing else but dust and heat and thirst and
the pitiful bawling of the cattle.

Hour after hour the men urged the weary cattle
up the trail. Late in the afternoon the leader of
the herd smelled water ahead. He lifted his head
and let out a mighty bellow. At once the whole
herd broke into a wild stampede.

The men let the cattle go. There wasn't a thing the cowboys could do anyway.

"Well," said John, "at least they are headed the right way this time."

The men rode along watching the herd. Then three shots rang out over the noise of the pounding hoofs. It was Boss Charlie's signal that something was wrong up ahead. The men let their horses feel the spurs.

They found Boss Charlie arguing with an ugly man holding a shot gun. Behind the man was a fence surrounding a water hole.

The fence was different from any John had seen before. It was made of strands of wire twisted together. Every few inches along the entire length were sharp points, or barbs, of wire.

The lead cattle had run against the barbed-wire fence. The sharp points had cut deep into their flesh. Some of the cows were still tangled in the wire. Their efforts to free themselves only made matters worse. The barbed wire was ripping their hides and flesh into ribbons.

"The water hole is on my land!" the ugly man

was shouting. "If you want water for your herd, you'll have to pay for it."

"You have no right to the land," Boss Charlie replied. "My cattle must have water!"

"You'll deal with me." The man started to raise his shot gun.

Quick as a flash, Boss Charlie whipped his six-shooter from his belt. He fired and knocked the shot gun out of the man's hand.

For a second, the man stood still. He muttered something about Texas sharp shooters. Then he ran to a sod hut a short way off the trail.

"Boys," the boss ordered, "tear down that blasted fence!"

Ropes whirled and settled over the fence posts. Horses strained to the work of pulling the posts out of the ground. When the fence was removed, the cattle rushed to the water hole. While they drank, angry cowboys talked about the cruel wire fence.

"We have some barbed-wire fences in Texas," said one.

"Yes," said Boss Charlie, "and the barbed-wire

fence may mean the end of the open range."

John's breath caught in his throat. The end of the open range! He didn't say anything. But that night in camp he asked the boss, "Are there any barbed-wire fences in Wyoming?"

"Well, no—not yet," the boss answered. "Why?"

John smiled happily. "That is where I'll have my ranch some day."

"So you want to be a cattleman. It takes money to buy a herd and run a ranch, John."

"I know it. I'm saving my money. Some day I'll be a cattleman."

"You have some pretty big ideas," spoke up Mac. "What's the matter with being a cowboy?"

"Not a thing in the world!" John laughed.

While the men were talking, a cry for help came from the night guards. The cattle were milling. The fear of a stampede sent the men galloping from camp.

Too late! The cattle streaked across the plains. Shouting cowboys raced through the starry night after the herd.

John, mounted on Golden, was riding with the

men. He leaned forward in his saddle. As he did, a sharp pain flashed through his body. Beads of cold sweat poured down his face. He felt like he was going to faint.

For a minute or two, John clung to Golden's neck. Then he slipped from the saddle and fell to the ground.

Golden stopped quickly and came back to where John had fallen. The horse brushed his soft nose against his master's shoulders.

"Get the boys, old fellow," John whispered. He tried to sit up, but fell back groaning.

Overhead the stars whirled in crazy circles. Then everything went black. John lay still in the dust of the trail.

———

Make up a short story of your own about cowboys on the trail. Begin with the cook calling the men to breakfast. Then tell what the cowboys did during the day. End your story with the cowboys singing at night around a campfire. Try to use all the cowboy words you can in your story.

Troubles on the Trail

HOURS later John awakened. Boss Charlie and the cook were sitting on the ground beside him. Toby was stretched out near by. When John stirred the dog came bounding forward.

"Where am I?" John asked.

"In camp," the boss answered. "You are a mighty sick cowboy, John."

"I'll be all right."

"You will be all right, if we get you to a doctor," the boss said. "If we don't, you'll die. Now, as luck would have it, we are not far from an army fort. We'll take you to the fort and leave you there with the army doctor."

"No! No! Take me with you."

"I can't, John. Your life is at stake."

With great effort John pulled himself up to a half-sitting position. "Take me with you, Boss," he pleaded. "I won't be any trouble. Honest, Boss. If I die—well, just bury me along the trail."

Boss Charlie turned to the cook. "What shall we do? I know how John feels about the trail."

"Let's take him," the cook answered. "I'll take care of the kid. He can ride in my wagon."

"Thanks," said John. "Thanks." As sick as he was, he fell back smiling.

For several days, John lingered between life and death. Part of the time, he almost wished he could die. By turns, he shook with chills and burned with a high fever. He couldn't eat or drink. He couldn't sleep.

It was agony to ride on the floor of the chuck wagon. The cook tried to drive carefully. But the trail was rough and the wagon rattled over the bumps. John had to bite his lips to keep from crying out in pain.

Then at last, the fever broke. The chills stopped. The pain left. John had won his fight to live.

John thanked the cook for taking care of him.

The cook only laughed and said, "Forget it, Cowboy."

"Forget it!" John exclaimed. "Why, I can't! You saved my life. I'll always be grateful to you."

"All right, be grateful. But keep it to yourself. First thing you know, the boss will have me doctoring the sick cows."

The cook patted John on the shoulder. "Well," he said, "I have to fix the chow now. Anything I can do for you?"

John glanced around the wagon. "Where is my bag of clothes?"

"It's here with the other bed rolls and bags. Why?"

"I have some books in mine. I'd like to read awhile."

The cook found the bag and gave it to John. Then he jumped down from the wagon, and set to work cooking the noonday meal.

Shortly before noon, Boss Charlie rode into camp. "How is John?" he asked.

"Take a look," the cook replied. He pointed to the wagon. John was sitting propped up with blankets at his back. He was reading a book. Toby was lying beside his master.

"Howdy, Boss," John called. His voice was not very strong, but it was full of cheer.

The boss galloped to the wagon. "Howdy, Cowboy," he smiled. "Howdy."

As the other men rode into camp, their first question was, "How is John? How is the kid today?"

"Ask him yourself." The cook went on with his work.

The men reined in their horses and dismounted. They hurried to the chuck wagon to talk to John.

"Sure, I'm feeling fine," John told them. "I'll be on the job as soon as I can ride."

The men looked at John with surprise. They had all thought that he would die. Only his game spirit had pulled him through. He was thin as a post and yellow as corn bread. But here he was already eager to be working with them again.

"Come and get it!" the cook called. "Come and get it or I'll throw it out!"

Laughing and talking, the men ate their noon-day meal. Then they mounted fresh horses and rode out to the herd again.

"So long, John," they called. "See you later."

When John was better, he and the cook became good friends. John wanted to help with the meals. The big, rough man refused.

"No," he said. "But I'll tell you one thing you can do. Why don't you read to me while I work?"

John laid aside the book he was studying. He picked up another book and began to thumb through its pages.

"This is a good sea story called *The Pilot*," he said. "James Fenimore Cooper wrote it."

"He sounds like a regular fellow. Go ahead. Read it."

Now along the Chisholm Trail, cook and cowboy shared the story of the sea. Together they followed the hero, Long Tom Coffin, on his daring adventures.

The cook was so excited by the story that on two days the men had to eat burned corn bread. Perhaps they were too hungry to notice. Then again, it might have been because the cook patted his six-shooter.

One evening John said to the men, "I'm not

strong enough yet to stay on a horse all day. But I can take my turn at night guard duty."

"Wait a few more days," said the boss.

"Night riding is easy," John insisted. He smiled and added, "I'm sure the cows miss my singing."

"Well," the boss laughed, "I guess they do. They haven't stampeded since you have been sick."

The cowboys roared with laughter, and John laughed with them. Then he left camp, saddled Golden, and rode out to the herd.

In a week John was back at his regular position as point rider. It was good to be on the job again and to be doing his share.

By this time, the men were in Kansas. They had stopped to buy supplies in a little town just over the border from the Indian country. Then they had set out once more. They took a trail which led northwest across the rolling, grassy country toward Hays.

In the old days, the cowboys had driven their herds straight north on to Abilene. But the trail was closed when farmers began to take over this part of the state. The cattle trade moved farther west.

The trail to Hays was easy to follow. Boss Charlie and his men kept the herd moving.

One afternoon, they came to a small stream. The current was slow. The water was not very deep.

"We can cross before dark," the boss said. "It won't take more than an hour or two. Come on, boys, let's go."

What started out to be an easy crossing became one of the toughest on the trail. Halfway across the stream, the herd ran into quicksand.

The leading cattle were caught in the sandy trap. They bellowed in terror while they fought to free themselves. They could not, and they began to sink deeper into the loose sand.

Cowboys, ever ready for trouble, snapped into action. Some drove the rest of the herd across the stream. Others worked to rescue the trapped animals.

Whirling ropes flashed out and settled over the heads of the cattle. Men and horses had to use all their strength to pull the bellowing, frantic cattle to safety.

The men worked at great speed. But they did not save all the cattle. Ten cows were sucked down by the quicksand. Slowly the water closed over their heads, leaving no trace of the death trap.

It was long after dark when the cowboys had the whole herd across the stream. The cattle bedded down at last only to stampede later in the night. By the time the men rounded up the herd again it was daylight.

Weary men and weary cattle pushed on up the trail. Along the way, they passed the sod hut of a pioneer family. The next day, they passed the sod hut of another family.

That night in camp Mac said, "This place is plumb full of people. I wouldn't live here for a million dollars."

"I wouldn't either," a cowboy agreed. "Give me the open range and a horse to ride."

"Farmers and cowboys just don't get along together," said Boss Charlie. "Give a farmer a few acres of land, and he can make a living for his family."

The men were angry at the settlers. Fields of grain meant less grazing land for their herds of cattle. Barbed-wire fences meant fewer water holes.

John listened to the men talk. At last he motioned to Mac. "It's time for our stretch at guard duty."

The two men mounted their horses and left camp. They took over the night watch. As usual, they sang as they circled the sleeping herd.

Once John thought he heard men talking. He pulled Golden to a stop and listened.

Far away a coyote howled from the top of a low hill. All else was quiet.

And yet for some reason John sensed danger in the air. He could not understand why he was uneasy.

The sky was clear. Stars twinkled like bright jewels. The breeze was soft. There was no hint of a storm.

"I guess that I just imagine something is

wrong," John said to himself. He touched Golden lightly and rode on.

He could hear Mac singing as they neared each other. John took up the song.

> "Oh, a ten dollar horse
> And a forty dollar saddle,
> And I'm all set
> To punch Texas cattle.
>
>
> Come-a ti yi yipee
> Yipee yeh!
> Come-a ti yi yipee
> Yipee yeh! Yipee yeh!"

Sometime about midnight, the cattle began to stir. It was their habit to get up for awhile each night. Usually the herd bedded down again without any trouble.

Tonight the cattle did not bed down. They moved about restless, uneasy.

Suddenly the crack of a six-shooter rang out. A man shouted, "Cut off the leaders! Let the rest go!"

The gun blazed again. The herd broke into a wild stampede.

"Cattle rustlers!" John gave Golden the spurs.

Ahead in the darkness, John could see the black outline of the herd streaking across the plains. He could hear men shouting, but he could not see them.

In a few minutes Boss Charlie and his cowboys came galloping from camp. With John in the lead, the men overtook the herd. The rustlers were gone. Hard work and fast riding ended the stampede.

While the men circled the herd John and Mac told Boss Charlie what had happened.

"It was a gang of cattle rustlers all right," said John. "I heard one shout, 'Cut off the leaders! Let the rest go!' I'm afraid we will find some cattle missing."

"Yes, I'm sure we will," the boss replied.

"I'd like to catch those rustlers," said Mac.

"So would I," the boss said. "We'll count the herd in the morning. If we haven't lost too many cows, we're going on."

"But the rustlers, Boss!" exclaimed John. "We can't let them get away with our cattle."

"We have no time to waste looking for them. We still have a long way to go."

"You're the boss. We'll do whatever you say."

"We have had plenty of bad luck on this drive," said Mac.

The boss shrugged his shoulders. "It could be worse," he replied. Then he smiled a little. "This is the long trail, boys. Follow it, and you learn to take the bad luck with the good."

The boss gave his horse the spurs and rode on. He started to sing the "Old Chisholm Trail."

"Now, how do you like that!" exclaimed Mac. "Boss Charlie's singing is enough to scare the daylights out of a pack of coyotes."

John laughed. "Let him scare the coyotes. But we better warn him to stay away from the cows."

Land of Ropes and Saddles

AT daylight, the herd was counted. The rustlers
had run off with thirty longhorns. But Boss
Charlie gave orders for the drive to begin.

The men pushed on to Hays. A few miles from
town the cowboys made camp. In the evening
the cattle were bedded down earlier than usual.

Most of the men were riding to Hays. Laughing
and talking, they pulled out their bags of clothes
and dressed for a night in town.

"Have a good time," Boss Charlie told them.
"But don't get into trouble."

The boss could just as well have talked to the
wild Texas longhorns. After lonely months and
hard work on the trail, the cowboys wanted to
have a good time.

And they had a good time! Whooping, hollering,
they raced their horses up and down the streets

of the town. They danced in the crowded dance halls. Their silver spurs jingled with every step.

In true cowboy fashion, they spent their money freely. When it was gone, they returned to camp still whooping and hollering.

The cattle drive started again. The trail led north to the sun-baked country of Nebraska. The grass was crisp and brown. The ground was hard as rock. Most of the water holes were dry.

Late one afternoon, Boss Charlie was riding with John at point position. The two men were talking about the cattle business.

While they rode along, John noticed the herd was restless. The cattle were shaking their heads.

"What's the matter with them?" John asked himself.

He looked around. On the trail ahead a gray veil hung across the country. It might be smoke. A gust of hot air hit his cheek.

"Boss," John shouted, "it's a prairie fire! A prairie fire!"

Boss Charlie's face went white. But his voice was steady as he said, "We're in for it, John."

He whipped the six-shooter from his belt. He sent three quick shots into the air.

"Turn the herd!" he called. "Turn the herd!"

John gave his horse the spurs. The cowboys in the rear came galloping up to help.

Fear swept through the herd with the speed of the flames. Wind came with the fire, driving it faster and faster through the dry grass. Orange-colored flames danced like greedy tongues.

The fire ran along the ground burning everything in its path. Black, choking smoke rose to the sky.

The herd plunged ahead. The cattle were mad with fear. They were racing straight toward the raging flames.

The cowboys tried to turn the animals. The men spurred their horses to greater speed. They rode along the very edge of the fire.

At last the leading cattle were forced to turn. Habit made the others follow. The flames swept by.

The cowboys sang as they circled the herd. The cattle quieted and bedded down for the night.

There was still a chance, however, that they might stampede. Extra men were put on guard duty. In camp, every cowboy slept with the reins of his night pony in his hands.

The night passed without any trouble. At dawn, the camp was awakened by the cook calling, "Come and get it! Come and get it or I'll throw it out!"

The cowboys kept the herd moving. The days were hot—scorching hot.

The cattle had not had water for several days. Suffering from thirst, they lagged along the trail. Then they began to stagger and bump into one another. The herd had gone blind!

John watched the trail ahead for a sign of Boss Charlie. At last the boss came riding over a low hill.

John raced forward. "The herd has gone blind," he reported.

"I was afraid of that," Boss Charlie replied quietly. "Well, all we can do is to stay on the trail."

The cowboys kept the bawling longhorns moving. The only chance to save the cattle was to get them to a water hole. If the cattle could drink plenty of water, soon they would be able to see again.

The terrible day of suffering dragged on. The sun set. A light breeze began to blow across the plains. Would the breeze bring the smell of water to the suffering cattle?

John watched the leaders of the herd. All at once they stopped in their tracks. They lifted their heads and smelled the air. Then with a bellow they broke into a trot.

"Water!" John shouted to the rider behind him. "They have smelled water!"

"Water!" Cowboy yelled to cowboy. "Water!"

The herd stumbled over the trail. Cowboys guided the blind animals to the water hole.

In the morning, the cattle could see again. The men spent two days at the water hole. On the third morning, the cows were rounded up and the drive went on.

A few days later, the cowboys came to the old Oregon Trail. The trail was a busy one before a railroad was built across the country.

Thousands of settlers had traveled over the famous old trail to the Pacific coast. Some went to California to mine for gold. Others were seeking rich lands for farms. They did not like the great plains country. The plains country, they said, was fit only for Indians and buffalo.

Then one fall, some traders were caught in the early snows of Wyoming. They had no feed for their ox teams. And so the animals were turned loose on the plains. The traders were sure the oxen would die during the long, cold winter. But in the spring, the oxen were in good shape.

"How could the animals have lived?" the traders asked. "How?"

The rich grass was the answer. And there were miles and miles of grazing land. Why, this country would be a wonderful place to raise cattle!

The news spread. And up from the south came Texas cowboys with herds of wild longhorns. At last, the great plains country was good for something. It was new cow country.

Boss Charlie and his cowboys followed the Oregon Trail for many miles. Day after day, they kept the herd moving. The country began to change. The men were coming into the high plains of Nebraska. Farther west, the hills rose higher and higher.

The cowboys were nearing the end of their long, long trip. Beyond the hills lay Wyoming.

With Boss Charlie in the lead, the men headed for the hills. The next day they rode into the Wyoming country.

The beauty of Wyoming made John hold his breath. Never, he told himself, would he forget this day.

Far away, the Rocky Mountains rose to a blue, sunny sky. Endless miles of rich grazing land stretched on and on.

"It's beautiful," John thought. "And best of all, this is cow country."

One night in camp, Boss Charlie said, "We are almost there, boys. Tomorrow, we will reach my ranch on Running Water Creek."

"Yipee!" the cry went up around the campfire.

Men shouted and danced. Mac brought out his fiddle and struck up a tune. As the men sang, a

touch of sadness came into their tired voices.

John was thinking of the long, long trip up the trail from Texas. He knew the men were thinking of the drive, too.

The drive had begun in March. Now it was the middle of August. For five and a half months, the men had shared every danger, every hardship.

The trail drive of fifteen hundred miles had been packed with adventure. Stampedes! River crossings! Rustlers! A prairie fire! A blind herd bellowing for water!

John thought of Rusty and Packsaddle. He missed them both. They were top hands as cowboys. They were top hands as friends.

"Fellows," spoke up Mac, "this is a new song. I'm not sure of the words. But it goes something like this:

'Whoopee ti yi yo, little dogies, whoopee yo,
 It's your misfortune and none of my own.
Whoopee ti yi yo, little dogies, whoopee yo.
Wyoming is now your new home. Whoopee yo!' "

Mac sang the chorus several times. The men

joined in, and their voices rang through the starry night.

"I like that song," said John. "It sounds just right."

"It's a good song," a man agreed. "But the 'Old Chisholm Trail' beats them all."

"You're right, there," John smiled. "I suppose it will always be our favorite. But I like the new song, too. I guess that's because Wyoming already seems like home to me."

"Are you going to stay up here?" a cowboy asked.

John nodded. "This is where I am going to spend the rest of my life."

Boss Charlie looked at John and smiled. "It doesn't take you long to decide what you want to do. Does it?"

"No," John grinned.

"Why have you decided to stay here?" the boss asked.

John threw back his head and laughed. "This is cow country," he answered. "This is the land of ropes and saddles."

Yankee Weather

Boss Charlie and his cowboys reached the ranch at sunset. The cook and Toby were already there. Supper was almost ready.

The herd was turned out to graze. Horses were penned in the big corral. Bed rolls were tossed up on dusty bunks in the bunk house.

The men went to bed early. The drive was over. The excitement was gone. Now for the first time, the men knew how tired they were, how hard the trip had been.

Once in the night, John was awakened by a noise. The cattle were stampeding—or so he thought. He sat up, grabbed for his boots only to find Toby had jumped up on his bunk.

The dog nosed his way under the blankets. John laughed softly, patted Toby, and fell asleep.

The cowboys were up at dawn. They rounded

up the cattle and drove them to the open range. The herd was turned loose for the winter months.

As the men rode back to the ranch one said, "Well, our work is done. I guess I'll drift back to Texas."

"I'm going with you," said another. "I don't want to stay here and freeze to death in a blizzard."

The cowboys talked over their plans. Some wanted to return to the cow towns along the trail. A few planned to drift down to Cheyenne and spend the winter in town.

Each fall, the cowboys faced the same problem. There wasn't enough work to keep all of them busy during the winter months. They were on their own. They drifted from one place to another, waiting for the grass to turn green again. Then in the spring, they went back to their old outfits or to other ranches in the cow country.

Boss Charlie would need only two or three men during the winter. John hoped that he would be asked to stay.

"I want to work this winter," he told himself.

"But I can't expect the boss to keep me on the job. After all, I'm the youngest man in the outfit. I'll hang around awhile longer. Then if the boss doesn't ask me to stay, I'll drift on to another ranch."

Days passed and the boss said nothing about his plans. At last, John thought of a way to stay at the ranch. He would work all winter without pay. Before he could make his offer the boss sent for him.

"I'm leaving for Texas in a few days," the boss said. "I'll be back sometime next summer with my family. While I am gone, I must have a foreman in charge of my ranch."

John nodded.

"Who do you think would make a good one?"

John named several of the older cowboys.

Boss Charlie shook his head. "They are good," he replied, "but I can't depend upon them. Every pay day they race to the nearest town, spend all their money, and come back broke."

"Well," John smiled, "most cowboys think that is fun. Our life is pretty lonely, you know. We don't get many chances to have a good time."

"You don't spend your money, even when you get the chance."

"That's different," John said quickly. "I'm saving my money. I know what I want."

"So do I. I want you to be the foreman of my ranch, John. Will you take the job?"

At first, John was too surprised to answer. Then a broad grin spread across his face. "Of course, I'll take the job," he said. "I'll do my level best to be a good foreman."

"I know you will. By the way, don't you want to know what your pay will be?"

John laughed a little. "I'd forgotten all about that. You see, I was going to ask you to let me stay on here without pay."

"You mean you were willing to work for just your room and board?"

"Yes, and I'll still do it, Boss."

"That's mighty fine of you. But I can't let you do it. Your pay is thirty dollars a month."

"Thanks," John grinned.

"Now, let's talk business," said the boss. "I think

you can get through the winter with the help of one man. Which one of the boys of the outfit do you want?"

"I'd like to have Mac stay with me."

"All right. I'll keep him on the pay roll."

The boss talked on about the work to be done on the ranch. Since only a few horses would be needed, the rest were to be sold in Cheyenne. John was to buy more horses when the cowboys returned to work in the spring.

The boss warned John about the terrible blizzards which often swept the plains. He told about the soft, dry wind, which usually followed a blizzard. The wind was called a "chinook." It was a life saver to the cattlemen. It came from over the Rocky Mountains and melted the snow like magic.

When the boss finished he said, "Well, John, I'm leaving everything up to you. You have good cow sense."

John grinned. "I'm glad I'm a cowboy or I would think you were insulting me."

A few days later, Boss Charlie, the cowboys,

cook, and horses left the ranch. John and Mac watched the outfit ride away.

The golden fall days passed quickly. John and Mac were busy from morning till night.

They rode the range keeping track of their cattle. They put up hay for their horses. They repaired the ranch buildings and mended the gates and fences.

They lived in a log cabin instead of the bunk house. It was smaller and easier to heat. They chopped down trees and stacked the wood near the door of the cabin.

In November, the winter snows began. After each snowstorm, John and Mac rode out to drive the cattle back to their range.

"I wonder if this was a blizzard," John would say each time.

"It must have been," Mac always replied. "I never saw so much snow in all my life."

They would laugh, thinking of the first snow of the season. They thought a blizzard had struck the plains. They worked like mad piling enough wood in their cabin to last for several days. Then all at once, they saw that it had stopped snowing.

"Well, I'll be a dogie's uncle!" Mac had snorted. "You just can't depend upon this Yankee weather. A good old Texas norther won't let you down like this. No, sir!"

Then at last, a blizzard swept the plains country. John and Mac were forced to remain in their cabin. The wind moaned down the chimney and pulled at the leather door latch. Hungry wolves and coyotes howled close by. Toby, stretched out in front of the stove, growled at his unseen enemies.

The blizzard ended almost as quickly as it began. The gentle chinook blew in and melted the snow. All was well again in the cow country.

One morning, John saddled Golden and rode out on the range. He spent the day riding around to be sure his cattle were all right. He did want the herd to come through the winter in good shape.

"I'm a foreman now," he said to himself. "And I must make good. But so much depends upon the weather."

Late in the afternoon, John headed for home. Golden raced along a trail.

When they were still far from the cabin, the wind began to howl. It started to snow. The wind whipped the snow through the air with stinging force.

John pulled his red handkerchief up over his mouth and nose. He might just as well have covered his eyes, too. The snow was falling so thick and fast he could not see.

Fear gripped his heart. He was lost—hopelessly lost in a world of snow and wind. He leaned low on Golden's neck.

"We're caught in a real blizzard. I'm lost," he said. "It's up to you to get us home."

Golden bowed his head before the fury of the storm. Slowly the faithful horse plowed ahead.

Now John knew why Boss Charlie had warned him of the dangers of a blizzard. No man afoot could live long in the terrible storm. Wind stabbed into him like knives, even through his heavy coat and chaps. Flakes of snow cut his face.

Golden kept going straight into the blizzard. At last, he stopped.

John let the horse rest a few minutes and then

said, "Come on, old fellow. We can make it."

But Golden stood still. For a brief moment, the wind blew a clear place in the air and John saw a fence post. They must be home!

John slipped from the saddle. By following the fence, he was able to lead Golden to the barn.

With cold, stiff hands, John removed Golden's bridle and saddle. Then he brushed the horse and put a blanket on him.

"Thanks, old pal," he said. He flung his arms around Golden's neck and hugged him. "Thanks for bringing me home."

After John fed Golden and the other horses, he started for the log cabin. It was only some fifty or more feet from the barn. But in the blinding snow he could not see the cabin.

He knew the way, however, and so he pushed ahead. He kept one hand held out before him, hoping to touch the rough logs.

Slowly he made his way through the whirling, blinding snow. All at once he knew that he must have gone by the cabin. For a moment panic seized him. He stood still.

"Keep your head," he told himself. "Don't go around in circles. Figure this out carefully or you are a goner."

Now with both hands held out in front he took ten long steps to the left. He did not touch the cabin. Slowly, carefully, he took ten steps back to where he had started. Now he took ten steps to the right. No luck.

He took five steps forward, now five to the left. This would at least keep him from going around in circles. Surely he would soon find the cabin.

His legs and arms were growing numb. He was sleepy. He wanted to lie down and close his eyes. With every step the desire to go to sleep was becoming stronger. He knew what this meant.

The desire to sleep meant that his blood was flowing slower and slower. He was starting to freeze. Unless he found shelter soon, he would freeze to death. No man afoot could live long in a blizzard. No man afoot!

With all his will power, he fought against going to sleep. He forced himself to go on.

At last, John bumped into some logs. His heart

gave a leap of joy. It must be the cabin!

Then, as his hands felt downward, he knew he had bumped into the corral. His joy changed to black despair. Now he would have to start his search for the cabin all over again.

"Keep your head!" Over and over, he said the warning to himself. "Keep your head!"

John struggled on. His body was bent by the cruel, lashing wind. How much longer could he fight against the strange white world of snow and wind?

He staggered and fell flat on the ground. For a moment he lay still. Then he began to crawl along on his hands and knees.

His head knocked against something hard. His stiff, cold hands reached for the object and found it. What was it?

His numb brain told him it was pieces of wood stacked one on top of the other. Pieces of wood! The woodpile just outside the cabin door!

John let out a cry of joy. Slowly he pulled himself to his feet. The next thing he knew he was pounding on the cabin door. It opened. He stumbled inside to the blessed warmth and fainted dead away.

Hours later John came to life again. He was in bed, covered with blankets. Mac was standing over him.

"You're all right, fellow," Mac was saying to him. "You're all right now."

John nodded. "Yes, I'm all right," he spoke slowly. He forced himself to smile and added, "You know Mac, you can't depend upon this Yankee weather. I'll take a good old Texas norther any day."

---

1. How long did it take Boss Charlie and his cowboys to make the trail drive to Wyoming? How many miles did they travel?

2. The cowboys had many adventures on the trip. Tell about the one you thought was the most interesting and exciting.

3. Why did John decide to stay in Wyoming?

4. What is a chinook?

5. Tell what happened to John when he was lost in the blizzard.

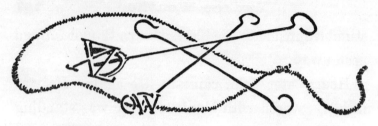

Riding, Roping Cowboys

THE rest of the winter passed with little more excitement. Snowstorms and blizzards raged and died away. Chinook winds blew and melted the snow and ice. The days grew longer, the sun warmer. Spring was on its way.

Early in April, a visitor came to John and Mac's cabin. The visitor was a young cowboy from a ranch some twenty miles farther south.

"We're mighty glad you can spend the night with us," said John.

"We certainly are," Mac agreed. He nodded toward John and laughed. "After spending a whole winter with that old coyote I'd welcome Jed Dorn."

"Jed Dorn?" questioned the cowboy. "Never heard of him."

"Dorn was a cattle rustler in Texas," John explained. "I made the mistake of telling Mac

198

about him. You know, on long winter nights there isn't much to do except to talk."

"Sure, I know," the cowboy replied. "And I'll bet a ten-gallon hat this jack rabbit does plenty of talking, too."

"Oh, no," Mac laughed.

"What about Katie?" John asked with a smile. "Wasn't she the little dancer in Hays?"

Mac grinned and shrugged his shoulders. "All right, partner, you win."

The men pulled their chairs up to the stove and sat down near it to keep warm. The visitor glanced around the room.

"Say, this is a pretty nice place," he said. "All fixed up with kerosene lamps, pictures, a bear rug, and everything."

"We are living in great style," John laughed. "This is Boss Charlie's cabin. The boss is in Texas now. He will return sometime this summer with his family. Then it's back to the bunk house for us."

"Are you foreman of this outfit?"

"Yes, I'm in charge," John answered. "Of

course, there hasn't been much to do during the winter. But we'll be plenty busy from now on."

"Yes, the spring roundup will soon begin," the visitor said. "And that is why I am here. I have the roundup orders for you."

"Orders?" questioned John. "Oh, yes. The boss said something about a few roundup rules."

"A few!" exclaimed the cowboy. "That's a good one!" He burst out laughing.

"What's so funny?" asked Mac.

"Stay here awhile and you'll find out," the cowboy grinned. "Why, brother, you can't shake a stick at all the laws we have up here."

"Who made all the laws?" asked John.

"The cattlemen of Wyoming," replied the cowboy. "And they sure run the cattle business in this country. They have laws for everything we do."

"Well," said John, "I don't want to break any laws. What are the orders?"

The cowboy explained the roundup orders. The range had been divided into districts. The ranches in each district carried out the same orders. The dates for the spring and fall roundups were set by law. Where the roundups started and where they ended was named by law.

"The spring roundup begins on the first of May," said the cowboy. "All the men in this district are to meet at my ranch. We will work together until we have rounded up the cattle. Those are the orders, boys. I guess I have told you everything."

"I'll carry them out," said John. "I don't want to get into any trouble. I'm going to have my own ranch here some day."

"Well, let me tell you something," said the cowboy. "Be honest and fair in all your dealings. Don't get mixed up with any shady—"

"You don't need to tell that to John," broke in Mac. "I don't know how you rate a top hand in Wyoming. But where we come from John Kendrick is a top hand in any man's outfit."

John held up his hand. "That's enough, Mac."

"I am only trying to help you fellows," the cowboy said. "As I told you, the cattlemen run this country. They keep close check on all cowboys.

Any cowboy who gets mixed up with rustlers is out of luck."

The men talked on, mostly about their work as cowboys. Before the evening ended, they were good friends.

In the morning, when the visitor left he said, "I'm glad you fellows made it to Wyoming. And, John, I hope you get that ranch. Maybe you will take me on as your foreman."

"You would be a good man," John smiled. "But I have already picked out a top hand for the job."

The cowboy laughed and swung into his saddle.

"Well, so long," he said as he gave his horse the spurs. "Be at my ranch the first of May."

"We'll be there," John called. He started back to the cabin. Mac followed.

"Say, John," asked Mac, "who is going to be your foreman?"

"You."

"Me?"

"Sure," John laughed, turning around. "Who else did you think it would be, you old coyote? We came up the trail together. Let's stick together the rest of the way?"

"It's a deal." Mac held out his hand. "Let's shake on it."

During the next few weeks, John had little time to think of the future. He was busy getting ready for the spring roundup.

The cook and most of the old cowboys of the outfit came back to work. They were put on the pay roll again. Other men were hired to take the places of those who did not return.

Horses were bought at a ranch which did a good business in selling half-broken, wild horses. Two extra men were hired to care for the horses on the roundup.

Food supplies were loaded into the chuck wagon. Bed rolls and bundles of clothes were piled in another wagon.

At last everything was ready. The outfit headed for the meeting place.

The cowboys were glad to be back on the job. They laughed and talked as they rode along.

The cook, too, was in high spirits. He had lost

none of his wild driving habits. He kept his teams at full gallop and the old chuck wagon rattled over the trail.

Toby, for he was part of the outfit, was riding with the cook. Every time they hit a bump, the dog barked with joy.

Spring had come again to the cow country. It was roundup time in the land of ropes and saddles.

More than a hundred cowboys had gathered at the meeting place. The chuck wagons and bed wagons made the place look like a tent town.

There was much visiting around the many campfires the first evening. John met most of his neighbors. In this range country, a man was a neighbor if he lived within a hundred miles.

One man came over to John. "I'm general foreman in charge of the roundup," he said. "I work for the Wyoming cattlemen. Who are you and what's your outfit?"

"I'm John Kendrick. I'm foreman of Charlie Wulfjen's outfit up on Running Water Creek."

The man looked John over carefully. "You're pretty young to be a foreman," he said. "But I know Boss Charlie. I used to work for him in Texas. If you are his top hand, you're a good man to have around."

"Thanks," John replied. "This is my first job as foreman. I sure want to make good."

"I don't know why you shouldn't," the man said. "You're from Texas, aren't you?"

John smiled and nodded.

"Well," the man said, "so are most of the cows."

"That's true," John laughed. "But the way you handle this roundup business is new to me. I'm used to the cow hunts in the brush country of Texas."

"Well, our roundup is nothing more than a big cow hunt. We have to cover more country because our range is wide open. Often our cattle drift hundreds of miles. Outfits work together in order to get all their cattle."

The foreman slapped John on the shoulder. "Use plenty of cow sense. You'll get along all right."

"I'll do my best," John promised.

At dawn on the first day of May, the roundup

began. The general foreman divided the men into groups. Each group was to search a certain part of the country. Each group was to drive all the cattle to a selected spot.

Later, the men would cut out the cattle belonging to their outfits. Sometimes, the mavericks and calves were cut out and branded. Usually, however, they were driven to their home ranch and branded.

Every day from sunrise to dark the men were in their saddles. It was hard work, this roundup business.

John enjoyed every minute of every day. This was the life he loved. He was riding with men he admired. Brave and loyal they were, these cowboys of the range country.

At night tired, hungry men rode into camp. No matter how tired they were, the first thing they did was to care for their horses. Then each man would head for the chuck wagon of his outfit.

Usually the "old woman" had supper ready. If not, the men waited for the call, "Come and get it or I'll throw it out."

After supper, the cowboys visited with one another. They would sing and tell stories until it was time to turn in for the night.

The roundup lasted six weeks. When the men finished they had combed every mile of the rough country in their district. Thousands of cattle had been rounded up and returned to their owners.

The cattlemen took count of their herds and were pleased. They said the cowboys had done a good job.

A good job! Why not? Weren't they riding, roping cowboys?

"I never saw better riders in my life," John said to the roundup foreman. "I thought we were good in Texas. But my hat's off to the riders on this range."

"There is a saying that the riders come from the north," the foreman replied. "The ropers come from the south. But you can ride and rope with the best of them. You're a cowboy—a real cowboy, John Kendrick. My hat's off to you."

Cow Sense

LATE in August, Boss Charlie and his family arrived. John was able to give a good report to his boss. The herd was in fine shape. The new calves had all been branded.

"You have done a real job," Boss Charlie praised.

"This is cow country," John smiled.

"Do you still plan to make Wyoming your home?"

"Oh, yes!"

"I hope you will stick with me until you set up your own ranch."

"I will, Boss. You can count on me."

The next two years raced by. John was gaining fame as a young foreman who had good cow sense. Other ranches offered him higher wages to work for them. But John always refused.

"I'll double whatever you make here," one rancher said.

John shook his head. "Boss Charlie needs me. Mrs. Wulfjen is in poor health. Ranch life is too hard for her. Except for the summer months, the family lives in Cheyenne. And so most of the time I'm in charge of the outfit."

"I'll pay you three times what you are making now," said the rancher.

"No, thanks."

"Don't you need the money?"

"Sure, I do," John answered. "But it's not a question of money. It's a question of loyalty. I am Boss Charlie's foreman. He gave me a good break. I'm not going back on him."

It was only a few weeks later when Boss Charlie gave John another break. The boss wanted John to drive a herd of Texas longhorns to Wyoming.

"I'll do it," John said. "It will be fun to ride the trail again."

"How much money have you saved, John?"

"Well, not very much. But enough to buy three hundred head of cattle."

Boss Charlie laughed. "Do you always think in terms of cows?"

"Most of the time," John grinned.

"Why don't you buy some cattle of your own while you are in Texas?"

"It takes money to drive a herd up the trail. I haven't enough to buy a chuck wagon, hire a cook and some cowboys. No, I guess my cows will have to stay in Texas awhile longer."

"Buy your cows, John. My outfit can drive them up the trail with my herd. It won't cost you a cent."

"Do you mean it?"

"Why not?"

"Most cattlemen don't want their cowboys to own cattle," John replied. "You know, it's pretty easy for a cowboy to slap his brand on calves that belong to his boss."

"That's true," Boss Charlie agreed. "But you are honest. You work hard. Sometimes I think this is your ranch instead of mine. And another thing, John, I don't look upon you as one of my cowboys. You are my friend."

"I don't know how to thank you, Boss. All I can say is that I'll try mighty hard to keep your friendship."

In the spring of 1883, John was in Texas. He bought a big herd of cattle for his boss and hired ten cowboys and a cook. Then he bought his own cattle—his first herd. To be sure it was a small one. But he was now a cattleman!

Proudly he started up the long trail. The second trip was much like the first. There were the same old dangers: stampedes, river crossings, and trouble with settlers.

The trail was wider, deeper. New cow towns had sprung up where railroads crossed the trail. There were more small towns, more farms, and more barbed-wire fences.

There were many, many more herds on the trail. Most of the cattle were being driven to Wyoming. And the fact worried John.

"If this keeps up the Wyoming range will soon be too crowded," John thought. "Cows need grass and plenty of room. The cattle business may be ruined—even before I get started."

It took John and his cowboys six long months to make the trail drive to Wyoming. Tired, but happy, John reported to his boss.

While the men talked, Mrs. Wulfjen and the two girls listened quietly. After a long time Mrs. Wulfjen laughed a little. "Cows! Cows! Cows!" she said. "Tell me about Texas. Were the bluebonnets as beautiful this spring? Were the stars as bright at night?"

Cows, the long trail, and business were forgotten. For an hour or more, John and the Wulfjens talked about the old days in Texas.

"Those were happy days," Mrs. Wulfjen sighed. "Just thinking of them makes me feel better."

John smiled and nodded his head as though he agreed. But he wasn't thinking of the days gone by. He was thinking of the future.

"I may not become a big cattleman," he told himself. "But one thing for sure, it's all up to me."

John worked harder than ever now that he had his own herd. He rode in the fall roundup and stayed at the ranch all winter. Mac, and Toby, too, stayed with him.

The long winter dragged on, with its usual snowstorms and blizzards. But at last spring came. Creaking, old chuck wagons were greased and repaired. Whooping, hollering cowboys swung into their saddles. It was roundup time again in the cow country.

John's small herd had come through the winter in good shape. Many new calves trotted along beside their mothers.

Mac pointed to a mother cow with twin calves. "Kendrick luck!"

"It may be a good sign," John grinned.

One night during the roundup, John was talking to the foreman of the OW ranch. The OW Ranch belonged to a big outfit called the "Converse Cattle Company."

The owners of the company were smart business men. They had bought several ranches in the district, and they were trying to buy more.

Each ranch had its own foreman and cowboys. A range manager was in charge of all the ranches.

"We're a million dollar outfit," said the foreman.

John whistled. A million dollars!

"That's a lot of money to be tied up in cows," he said. "A long, severe winter could wipe your company out of business."

"Wipe the Converse Cattle Company out of business! Why, that couldn't happen!"

"Yes, it could," John said quietly. "The range is becoming too crowded. Cows need grass—plenty of it! If a severe winter strikes, there will not be enough grass for all the herds."

"Maybe so. But there is plenty of money in this cattle business. Men from New York, Chicago, and other Eastern cities are setting up ranches out here. Men from Scotland and England are flocking to this country."

"Yes," John laughed, "and half of them don't know a cow from a wild duck. But they sure have a good time playing cowboy."

The foreman laughed, too. "Yes, don't they? We have a young Englishman at the OW. He's the son of a lord or an earl or something. I don't go in for fancy titles. But he is a fine fellow. There he is now—over there at the campfire singing with the boys."

"Let's go over and sing with them," said John.

"Just a minute, John," said the foreman. "I have been watching you on this roundup. You have good cow sense. Why don't you sign up with my outfit?"

"Nothing doing," John replied. "My outfit suits me just fine."

"Well, all right. But if you ever need a job, you will find one waiting for you at the OW."

"Thanks. I'll remember."

Weeks later, the roundup was over. John and his cowboys returned to their ranch with their cattle.

One day, while John was branding his calves, Boss Charlie sent for him. John hurried to the log cabin.

Mrs. Wulfjen was sitting on the porch. She was smiling. John thought that he had never seen her so happy.

"Where are the girls?" he asked, stopping beside her chair.

"You mean my tomboys?" Mrs. Wulfjen laughed. "They are out riding on the ranch."

"Oh, that's right. I told Eula she could ride Golden today."

"You are very kind to let Eula ride Golden. I didn't know a cowboy ever let anyone ride his favorite horse."

"Well, sometimes even a cowboy lets his best friend ride his favorite horse."

John strode on into the cabin. Boss Charlie and the OW foreman were waiting for him.

"John," said Boss Charlie, "I'm selling my herd to the Converse Cattle Company. My wife is homesick. We are going back to Texas. I know about the OW offer. You better take it."

"I promised to stick with you, Boss."

"You're the best foreman I ever had or ever will have. But I wouldn't ask you to leave Wyoming. You love this country. Stay here, John. Make good."

"My company wants you at the OW," spoke up the foreman. "In fact, I can offer you a better deal now. I have been promoted. You can take over as foreman of the OW. Do you want the job?"

"Yes," John answered. "But I won't take it,

unless there is a job at the OW for Mac. Then, too, I want to bring my herd with me."

"You can run your cows on the OW range," the foreman replied. "But I'm not sure about a job for Mac. We have all the cowboys we need right now."

"Well, then count me out. Thanks for the offer anyway."

John slapped his hat on his head. He started toward the door.

"Just a minute," the foreman said. "We'll find a job for Mac, if that's what it takes to get you at the OW."

John turned quickly. "That is what it takes," he grinned. "I'll never sign up with an outfit that doesn't have a job for Mac. We came up the trail together. We're sticking together the rest of the way."

The Terrible Winter

THE Wulfjen family moved to Texas. John and Mac went to work for the OW outfit. The OW was bigger, but it was like other ranches where they had worked.

One day Mac said to John, "I like this place. I'm a loyal OW man already."

"So am I," John replied. "It's a good outfit. But I'll never find a better man to work for than Boss Charlie. I'll always be loyal to him."

"The boss is all right. Say, that was mighty nice of you to give Toby to little Eula. She and Toby were great pals."

"I did it for a very selfish reason. Toby is getting old. The winters up here are too cold for him. Now this winter while we are freezing, I'll think of him chasing around in the Texas sunshine. Good old Toby!"

"Good old Texas sunshine!" Mac grinned.

"Come on," John laughed. "Let's get to work."

John, as foreman, was always on the job. He rode and roped with his cowboys. He never asked them to do anything he could not or would not do himself.

Several times a year, John went to Cheyenne to report to the Converse Cattle Company. The range manager and the foremen of the other company ranches also had to report. The meetings were held at the Cheyenne Club.

John, of course, knew about the club. Who didn't? It was the most famous club in the West, and one of the best in the world. Only the wealthy cattlemen could afford to belong to it.

"This is some bunk house," John said to the range manager.

"Yes," the manager agreed. "We do all the work and the cattlemen live like kings."

"Well," John smiled, "I'm a cattleman and I—"

"You and those cows of yours!" the manager laughed. "I'll bet you know every cow and calf in the herd."

John laughed, too. "Sure I do," he answered.

The man was silent for a while. Then he said, "John, you have a good start. Some day you will be a big cattleman. And if I know men, you'll be one of the best in the business."

"Thanks."

John enjoyed the meetings at Cheyenne. He liked the men who owned the company.

"We hire top hands to work for us," the president of the company said to John. "How you manage your outfit is your business. All we care about are good reports."

At one meeting, John said he would like to move the OW outfit to northern Wyoming.

"It is all right with us," the president replied. "We don't care where our cattle graze. But why do you want to move? Your reports show that the OW is making money for us."

"We had a good year," John agreed. "But the range is too crowded. And to make matters worse settlers are coming into this country. I'd like to move farther north to get away from them and their barbed-wire fences."

"Have you some place in mind, Kendrick?"

"I'd like to move to the Powder River country. It's wonderful range country, sir."

The president nodded. "I have some friends who own big ranches up there," he said. "They are always boasting about the Powder River country. They have built regular castles for themselves and they live in great style."

"I hear that they have more servants than cows," John grinned. "But don't worry about the OW outfit. We're too busy for castles and fancy living."

The president laughed and slapped John on the shoulder. "Go ahead, Kendrick. Do whatever you think needs to be done. It's all up to you."

John lost no time in moving the OW outfit to northern Wyoming. The new ranch was located some fifty miles from Sheridan.

The Powder River country was ideal cow country. Why shouldn't it be? Long before the cowboys came riding up the trail this had been buffalo country. And wherever buffalo live, Indians live, too.

For years and years, this vast hunting ground had belonged to the Indians. The grassy, rolling country had been theirs until they lost it to the white men.

Now where buffalo had roamed, Texas long-horns grazed. Stagecoaches rattled over old Indian trails. Towns grew up where Indian villages had stood. Railroads cut across the land.

Once the majestic Big Horn Mountains had echoed with the war whoops of fighting Indian braves. Now the "Hi! Yi! Yi!" of riding, roping cowboys rang out instead. They had taken over the Powder River country.

"Hi! Yi!" John and his cowboys shouted. "Powder River!"

The first year at the new ranch was a good one. John's report was the best turned in at the company meeting.

John worked hard. He spent many long hours in the saddle. He had a fine string of sturdy cow ponies.

Golden was too old for the rugged life of a cow pony. But he was still John's favorite.

Often John saddled Golden, and rode out alone to study the country. He rode along the creeks and draws. He followed winding trails into the canyons. He covered every mile of the OW range. He wanted to know the places where the cattle would find shelter during winter storms.

John enjoyed the lonely trips. The beauty of the country never failed to stir him deeply. And yet he was uneasy, troubled. There was danger in the air.

The summer was hot and dry. The grass died early, too early for the cattle to be in good shape for the coming winter.

Early in August, John noticed birds flying south. Golden's coat was shaggy and thicker than it had ever been. The cattle, too, were shaggy.

"We're in for an early winter," John told his men. "I'm worried. Mac and I are staying at the OW. I'll keep any man on the pay roll who wants to work with us. I have a feeling we will have plenty to do this winter."

Ten cowboys signed up to stay at the ranch. The others left when the fall roundup was over.

A few weeks later, the first snow of the season covered the country. John and his cowboys waited until the storm ended. Then they swung into their saddles and headed south. Riding along, they looked for their herds which had drifted with the storm.

The cattle were found in deep draws, in canyons, and other sheltered places. Some had to be roped and pulled out of snow drifts.

At last, the cattle were rounded up. They were driven back to the OW range. Aching with weariness and stiff with cold, the men returned to their bunk house.

A day or two of mild weather followed. Then it turned cold again. A heavy crust of ice formed over the snow.

Cattle, with their divided hoofs, cannot paw through deep or crusted snow. They drift on, searching—searching for grass. If the range is deep in snow, the cattle drift on until they die from hunger and cold.

John and his cowboys rode out to their herds. The men scraped the crust from patches of snow.

Bellowing cattle pawed through the soft snow to the grass beneath.

Snowstorms came one after another. Each time the cowboys had plenty of hard, cold work to do.

In December, blizzards came sweeping down from the north. The OW men were forced to remain in their bunk house. John paced the floor, back and forth, back and forth.

"Sit down," Mac said. "There isn't a thing in the world you can do."

"I know it!" John threw up his hands in a helpless manner.

"I never saw a winter like this one," said a cowboy. "If the cattle live through it, I'll believe in miracles."

In January, a chinook blew in and melted the snow. Creeks and rivers were flooded. The range land, too, was covered with icy water.

Then the worst blizzard of all tore across the country. John and his cowboys dared not leave the bunk house. No man could face the storm and live.

Outside, it was thirty degrees below zero. Then it tumbled down—down to forty—to fifty—to sixty-three degrees below zero. Day and night, a howling wind blew with terrible force. The range was a frozen world of snow and ice.

John and his cowboys did not need to be told what was happening on the range. Too well they knew. Tragedy had struck the cow country!

Safe in their bunk house, the quiet group sat around the stove. They didn't do anything. There was nothing to do. They didn't say anything. There was nothing to say.

The blizzard finally blew itself out only to be followed by more snow, more blizzards. The long terrible winter of 1886-87 dragged on and on.

Not until the spring, did the men learn the full tragedy of the terrible winter. The entire cow country was a range of frozen death. Thousands —tens and tens of thousands of cattle had starved and frozen to death. They were found piled up in draws, in canyons, in valleys. Only a few still lived—only a few of the once great herds.

Roundup in the spring was always a gay time. But this spring, the cowboys rode the range in silence. And at night around their campfire, they did not sing and joke as in the good old happy days.

One night, John and Mac were sitting with a group of men around a campfire. The men were talking in low voices.

John did not say anything. Nothing could be gained by talking about the terrible winter. Now was the time to plan for the future. How long would it take to save enough money to buy another herd?

All at once a cowboy jumped to his feet. "I'm through," he said. "I've seen all the dead cows I ever want to see. Poor dumb animals. They depended upon us to take care of them. What did we do? Nothing! We aren't cowboys."

"I'm sure my company will agree with you," said John. "When I turn in my report I know I'll be out of a job. But that doesn't mean that I'm through with the cattle business."

"Still think you'll be a cattleman?" the cowboy asked.

John nodded.

"Don't forget your own herd was wiped out, Kendrick," spoke up a man. "Too bad you didn't spend your money with the rest of us. At least we had a good time. You're right back where you started."

"Well, what if he is?" Mac asked in anger. "Can't a man start all over again?"

"What good will it do? You can't win in this business."

"You're wrong there, Cowboy," said John. "If you don't give up when the going gets tough, you can win in any business."

A silence fell over the group. The dancing flames of the campfire lighted up the tired faces of the men.

At last a man said, "I guess you're right, Kendrick. But it takes plenty of courage to start all over again."

John smiled a little, the first time in days. "I'm not starting all over again," he said. "Sure I lost my herd. It was tough luck. But I've come a long way. I'm a better cowboy now than I have ever been. And I'll win—some day."

Girl of the OW

BEFORE the roundup ended, John received a letter from the company. He was told to come to Cheyenne at once with his report.

Leaving Mac in charge, John took a stagecoach to the cow town. As soon as he arrived he hurried to the Cheyenne Club.

The great rooms of the famous club were quiet. A pile of baggage stood near a door. John looked at the tags on the trunks and suitcases.

"Chicago. New York." he said to himself as he read the addresses on the tags. "England. France. Scotland."

Walking on he added, "The wealthy cattlemen are pulling out. Too bad. But then again maybe it isn't. Maybe it's a good sign."

He stopped before the door of the room where the company meetings were held. He stood there a minute looking at the report in his hands. Then he squared his shoulders, opened the door, and strode into the room.

The president and the foremen of the company ranches were seated at a long table. As John entered they turned in their chairs. They stopped talking.

John gave his report to the president. "I'm sorry, sir," he said. "Mighty sorry."

The president nodded. He didn't even look at the report. He just placed it on top of the other papers in front of him.

John sat down in his usual chair at the table. He glanced around. At other meetings, the men were full of noisy good humor. Today, they were silent, grim. No one spoke.

The president rose slowly to his feet. "It's all over, boys," he said in a low voice. "We're through."

Tired cowboys slouched in their chairs. Someone coughed. Another man crossed his legs. The spurs on his muddy boots jingled like tiny silver bells.

"My partners and I have lost a fortune," the

president went on. "We're quitting before we lose all our money. We're licked. We can just as well admit it."

The men began to pour out their troubles. They blamed the weather, the settlers, the crowded range.

"I guess this wasn't cow country after all," said a foreman.

John jumped to his feet. "This is cow country," he said. "It will always be cow country."

The foreman snorted. "Then why is our company going out of business?" he asked. "Why did most of the big companies go broke? Why are the wealthy cattlemen leaving?"

"They have no reason to stay," John replied. "To them the cattle business was an adventure or a quick, easy way to make money. But the cattle business really means something to us. It is our way of life. We have something to fight for, and if we fight, we can win."

The foreman shook his head. "We haven't a chance," he said. "We will never get over this terrible winter."

"Oh, yes, we will," John replied. "But it will take years of hard work. More than likely the cattle business will never be the same again. Times have changed. Settlers are—"

"Settlers!" the foreman exploded. "Settlers and their blasted barbed-wire fences! I never want to hear of them again."

"That goes double for me!" another man exclaimed. "The settlers will ruin this country. They are taking up claims of land."

"Yes," the foreman said. "That means there will be less grazing land for us. Year after year the range will become smaller."

"The boys are right, Kendrick," said the president. "The settlers are taking over. By law, the land they take will become their property."

"That's true," John agreed. "But is there a law against cattlemen owning land?"

"Well, no," the president replied.

"Of course, there isn't a law against us," said John. "All right then, let the cattlemen buy land, too."

The cowboys protested. But John stood his

ground. Quietly, earnestly, he went on talking.

"Ranches will be smaller," he said. "Better cattle must take the place of the wild Texas longhorns. Then, another thing, cattle must be fed during the winter. They must not be left to shift for themselves."

John leaned across the table. "This winter has taught us a bitter lesson," he said. "We trusted in luck too long. Let's get to work. Sure, I know we are up against it. The fight will be a tough one. But we can win, boys. This is cow country."

"By George!" the president exclaimed. "I think you are right, Kendrick. This is no time to quit. Let's fight it out together."

John's faith melted away the lost hope of the men like a gentle chinook melted snow. With a "Hi! Yi! Yipee!" the cowboys crowded around him. They slapped him on the shoulders. They shook his hands. They cheered and shouted.

"All right, boys," the president called, "let's get down to business. Our new range manager will give you his orders. Come on, Kendrick, take over. The job is yours."

John was taken by surprise. He stood still for a minute. Then he took his place at the head of the table beside the president. Another burst of cheers came from the cowboys.

A week later John was back at the OW. His men were proud that he was now range manager of the company. They were glad that Mac had been made foreman of the OW.

"You're the best outfit on the range," John told them. He turned to Mac. "Good luck, partner. Good luck."

John's new duties kept him very busy. The company ranches were far apart. He spent many long hours in the saddle riding from one ranch to another.

The OW was his favorite outfit. Under his able management the OW became a model ranch. Bigger and better corrals and barns were built. A comfortable, five-room log cabin was erected near the bunk house.

John lived in the cabin. It was his office, too. Here he wrote out long reports for his company.

Often alone at night, he sat at his desk working

on new plans. He could hear the cowboys singing in the bunk house. Sometimes he would join them, and sing with them for an hour or two. When they turned in for the night, he would walk back to his cabin and go to work again.

As range manager, John had to spend more time in Cheyenne than before. One day while he was there he received a letter from Boss Charlie.

"We're living in Greeley, Colorado, now," the letter read. "It's only fifty miles from Cheyenne. Why don't you come to visit us?"

John wanted to see his old friend. He finished his business with the company and then went to Greeley.

The visit was a happy one. From then on, John often visited the Wulfjen family.

After the fall roundup in 1890, John went to Greeley again. He was surprised at the change in Eula. She was no longer a tomboy, flying around with her hair in pigtails. Her hair was piled on the top of her head, and her skirts were long. She was a young lady of seventeen. She was trying very hard to act grown up. She walked with easy grace. She was beautiful, and John told her so.

"Thank you," she smiled up at him.

John's heart dropped straight down into his cowboy boots. He was in love.

"Eula" he said, "I remember the first time I saw you."

"Do you really, John?"

"Yes, you told me, that when you grew up, you would marry me."

"I was only a child," Eula blushed.

"I hope," John tried to keep his voice steady, "I hope you haven't changed your mind."

Eula placed a hand on John's arm. "I haven't," she whispered. "I still want to marry you."

A few months later, Eula and John were married. They spent their honeymoon in the East. They went to Chicago, Niagara Falls, New York, and Washington, D. C.

Then they returned to the West, and Eula became the "Girl of the OW." The cowboys adored her—one and all.

The years sped by, years of hard work and happiness for John and Eula Kendrick. When their first child, a daughter was born, more happiness came into their lives. They named their baby, Rosa Maye. But the cowboys usually called her "Little Girl of the OW."

Mac was devoted to the baby. He used every kind of excuse to spend all his free time at the cabin.

One day he said to John, "I have been thinking about the future. It is a lonesome life for women on a ranch. Maybe you ought to move to Sheridan."

John nodded. "I have been thinking about it, too. I want Rosa Maye to go to school, have friends, and—"

"She must grow up to be a lady," Mac broke in. "She can't learn to be a lady at the OW."

"Oh, yes, she can." Eula came into the room with the baby in her arms. "And another thing, it's fun to live on a ranch. Rosa Maye will think so, too. I am going to teach her to swim, to shoot, ride horseback, and—and everything."

"You call that being a lady!" Mac exclaimed.

John threw back his head and laughed. "Why,

Eula," he said, "I believe you're still a tomboy."

"No, I'm not," Eula smiled. "But I remember my own happy childhood. I want the same for Rosa Maye. Of course, I want her to grow up to be a lady. But I also want her to be strong and healthy, both in body and mind. I want her to be honest, loyal, and brave."

Eula lifted the baby high into the air. "Up-a-daisy, my little lady," she laughed. "Up-a-daisy!"

The very next day Rosa Maye's riding lessons began. At first she rode in her mother's arms. Then, when she could sit up, she rode on a pillow tied in front of her mother's saddle.

Almost every day Eula and the baby were out on the range. Sometimes, they would meet John and the cowboys coming in from a hard day's work.

When John went to Cheyenne, Eula and the baby rode to the stagecoach station with him. And when he returned, they were waiting there for him.

John was always glad to see them. Laughing and talking, they would ride back to the OW.

On one of his trips to Cheyenne, John had to

stay longer than usual. But as soon as he had finished his business, he started for home.

While the stagecoach rattled over the trail, John thought of the good news he had to tell Eula. He laughed aloud, thinking how happy she would be.

At last the stagecoach rolled to a stop. The "Girls of the OW" were waiting.

A few minutes later, the Kendrick family headed for the ranch. As they rode along, John said, "Eula, I have good news."

"What is it?" Eula asked. "Tell me."

"The OW is ours!"

"Ours?"

"Yes, I bought the ranch from the company. The OW is ours."

"Oh, John, how wonderful! After all these years you have your own ranch. I am so happy because I know what it means to you."

"Yes," John smiled. "My dream has come true. I still find it hard to believe. But the OW is ours, Eula. It's ours!"

At the top of a hill, they reined in their horses.

They did not speak. Silently, they looked out across the country they loved. To the west, the Big Horn Mountains stood guard over the miles and miles of grassy plains.

John took off his big, ten-gallon hat. With a sweeping wave, he motioned to the OW ranch buildings.

"This is our home, Eula," he said. "The OW is our outfit."

"Oh, John, I'm so happy I could cry." Eula bowed her head.

"Now isn't that just like a woman!" John laughed. He leaned from his saddle. He cupped Eula's chin in his hand.

"Girl of the OW," he said. "You're the top hand of this outfit."

———————

1. Why did the cowboys hate barbed-wire fences?

2. Why did John want to move the OW ranch to the Powder River country?

3. Tell about the terrible winter of 1886-87.

4. Why was John made range manager of the Converse Cattle Company? Was it an important job?

5. Who was the "Girl of the OW?"

Trail End

THE cowboys of the outfit cheered when John told them the good news. That night, the bunk house rang with their songs and laughter. No one had a better time than Mac, the new foreman of the OW.

"It's getting late, boys," Mac called. "But let's sing one more song."

The cowboys turned to John. "What will it be, Boss?" they asked.

"Let's make it the 'Old Chisholm Trail,'" John replied. "And say, Mac, tune up that old fiddle of yours for this song."

"All right, Boss," Mac grinned.

While Mac tuned the fiddle, John thought of the old trail. A flood of memories came rushing back to him.

He thought of Rusty and Packsaddle. They

were still top hands as real cowboys and true
friends.

In memory, John could again almost see the
long, weary miles of the trail. He could almost
smell the dust and feel the heat.

He heard again the pounding hoofbeats of
stampeding longhorns. Now came the riding,
roping cowboys galloping after the herd.

John was with the men. He was riding Golden
—the proud, wild leader of wild horses. And there
was Toby, too. Good old Toby!

Just then, Mac struck up the tune. John and
the men began to sing.

> "Come along my boys
> And listen to my tale,
> All about my troubles
> On the Old Chisholm Trail.
>
> Come-a ti yi yipee
> Yipee yeh!
> Come-a ti yi yipee
> Yipee yeh! Yipee yeh!"

The men sang many verses of the old song. Each time, during the chorus, they stamped their feet. Their boots sounded like horses trotting on the trail.

The song ended with a final, "Yipee yeh!" Soon all was quiet at the OW.

In the morning, bright and early, the cowboys were on the job. They saddled their horses and headed for the day's work on the range.

John and Mac watched them ride away. Then together, the two good friends went to John's office. Together, boss and foreman made plans for the OW and the future.

The years rolled by, bringing success to John Kendrick. Besides the OW, he now owned other ranches. He was one of the biggest and richest cattlemen in the West.

Success did not change John Kendrick. He was still all cowboy. He was never happier than when he was riding the range. And now he had a young son to ride with him.

The boy's name was Manville. He was a sturdy lad, and John was proud of him. Manville was a

good horseman. Why shouldn't he be! His mother
had taught him to ride just as she had taught the
"Little Girl of the OW."

The ranch was a wonderful place to live. The
children were free to do almost as they wished.
But they had school lessons to study. They had
a good teacher—their pretty, young mother.

One day, when the lessons were finished, Eula
said, "This is the last day of school. It's time for
vacation."

"Hi! Yi!" the children shouted. "Yipee!"

Eula smiled. "I have something else to tell you.
Your father and I think it is time for both of you
to go to a real school. We are moving to Sheridan."

"Oh, no, Mother!"

"Oh, no, Mother!"

"We are moving to Sheridan," Eula said again.
"We are going to build a fine new home there.
Won't you like that?"

"No," the children answered. "We like it here.
The OW is the best place in the whole world."

"I think so, too. We'll come back every summer
to the OW."

In the fall, the Kendrick family moved to Sheridan. There on a hilltop, the Kendricks built their home. It was a beautiful stone mansion, almost like a palace. The grounds around the mansion were like a big park, with trees and flowers.

John named the place "Trail End." He was proud of it. It was more than just a house to him. Many years ago he had followed a trail to become a cattleman. This was the end of the long trail. Here he wished to spend the rest of his life.

John often rode out to his ranches. But he spent most of his time in town. He became a business man. He was honest and fair.

John's name spread all over the state. In 1914, he was elected governor of Wyoming.

"It is a great honor to be governor," Eula told him. "I am proud of you, John, very proud."

John smiled, but made no reply. He walked to a window in the living room of the Kendrick mansion. He looked out over the country. Far away he could see the grazing lands of his ranches.

He stood quietly for awhile. Then he turned to Eula and said, "Yes, it's an honor. But it takes me away from all I love. We will have to move to Cheyenne, you know. I would rather stay here."

"Serve your state as governor, John," said Eula. "And when your term is over, we'll come back here."

A few weeks later the Kendricks moved to the governor's mansion in Cheyenne. One day John was walking to the capitol. He noticed an old cowboy standing on the steps of the building. When John was near, the cowboy hobbled away.

At first John didn't know the man. Yet there was something about him which made John think they had met before.

"Who is he?" John asked himself. "Who?"

Then John knew the answer. "Lopez!" he called. "Lopez!"

The cowboy stopped dead in his tracks. He turned and took off his big hat.

John hurried to meet his old friend. They shook hands warmly.

"You no forget," Lopez said over and over. "You big, rich man. Still you no forget."

"What are you doing?" John asked.

Lopez shrugged his shoulders. "No work for old cowboy on ranch."

John took a piece of paper from his coat pocket. He wrote something on the paper and handed it to Lopez. "Give this to Mac."

"I no understand."

"Mac is my friend," John went on to explain. "He lives at my ranch, the OW. Go to him. Give him this note."

"What you say to him?"

"I told Mac that you are an old friend of mine."

"He give me job?"

John shook his head. "Younger men are in the saddle now, Lopez."

"Then why I go to OW?"

"There are some other old cowboy friends of mine living at the OW," said John. "I want you to live there, too. The OW will be your home, Lopez. I will take care of you the rest of your life."

"You do this for me." Lopez choked. "For certain, you are my good friend." His bent shoulders began to shake. He turned away with a half sob. "For certain."

Slowly, John walked on to the capitol. He was thinking of the winter when he and Lopez had ridden the line together. That was long, long ago.

John turned and looked back. Lopez was gone. Already he was on his way to the OW.

John, as governor, had little time to give to his own business. He longed for the day when his term would end. He wanted to go back to the life of a cattleman.

Wyoming, however, had other plans for John Kendrick. Before his term as governor was over, he was elected to the United States Senate.

John went to Washington, D. C. Years passed. Senator Kendrick was an important, respected man in the Congress of the United States. Presidents were his friends. With honor he served his country and his state.

In the fall of 1933, when Congress adjourned, John returned to his home in Sheridan. He was tired, very tired. He was glad to be home again.

At sunset one November day, he was standing

at a big window of Trail End. He was looking out over the country he loved so well. There were the same old mountains guarding the rich valley. There were his fine herds of cattle grazing on his lands.

He heard Eula come into the room. He turned and smiled at her. "I'm going out to our favorite ranch tomorrow," he said. "Will you go with me, 'Girl of the OW?'"

Eula laughed. "Of course I will, Cowboy."

John did not go to the OW—ever again. Death came to him swiftly at his beloved Trail End.

*   *   *   *

Wealth and honor did not change the orphan boy who followed the long, long trail to success. John Kendrick lived and died a cowboy. He was loyal to his outfit. He never broke his word. He never forgot a friend. He was a top hand.

Word List

Abilene—**Ab' e leen**

canyon—**kan' yon**

chaps—shaps

Cheyenne—**Shi' an**

chinook—**chih nook'**

Chisholm—**Chiz' um**

chuck—chuk

chute—shoot

corral—**koh ral'**

coyote—**ky' ote**

dogie—**doh' gee**

Eula—**U' la**

gully—**gul' ee**

holster—**hol' ster**

lasso—**lass' oh**

Lopez—**Lo' pez**

maverick—**mav' er ik**

mesquite—**mess' keet**

mustang—**muss' tang**

rustler—**rus' ler**

stampede—**stam peed'**

stirrup—**stih' rup**

Whoa Haw—**Woh Haw**

Wulfjen—**Wolf' jen**

Wyoming—**Wy oh' ming**

Yipee—**Yip' pee**